THEOREM

For Pier Paolo Pasolini, post-war Italy was overrun by the corrosive forces of consumerism, bourgeois uniformity and shallow bourgeois conventions. In his writing and film-making he was frequently critical of the establishment. Condemned by those in power as dangerous and offensive to public morality, he remained, nevertheless, an extremely popular and influential figure. Through his work, he attempted to awaken people to a different set of values, both traditional and revolutionary.

A mystical and Marxist work, *Theorem* concerns a handsome, versatile young man who bewitches a wealthy middle-class family living in Milan. His sexual, emotional and intellectual hold over them is complete. When he abandons them, their desolation catapults each member of the family into a new life.

Published in 1968, *Theorem*'s rejection of conventional morality caused a public outcry. It deals with many of Pasolini's principal themes – the rejection of accepted morality in order to free oneself, the revolutionary power of the divine as opposed to the Church and the importance of individual as opposed to collective awareness. Remarkable in content and style, *Theorem* was written and filmed simultaneously; the action of the novel is seen as through the eye of a camera, resembling a scenario in form.

PIER PAOLO PASOLINI

Pier Paolo Pasolini is known primarily for the films he began making in the 1960s, the most famous of which are *The Gospel According to St Matthew, Theorem, The Decameron, The Canterbury Tales, Arabian Nights* and *Salò*. He was also a remarkable poet, and won fame and notoriety with his two Roman novels, *Ragazzi di vita* and *Una vita violenta*. In 1975 he was murdered by a homosexual prostitute.

The Letters of Pier Paolo Pasolini, Volume I 1940–1954 and *A Dream of Something*, a novel, are also published by Quartet Books.

PIER PAOLO PASOLINI

Theorem

Translated from the Italian and with an
Introduction by STUART HOOD

QUARTET ENCOUNTERS

Quartet Books

First published in English in Great Britain
by Quartet Books Limited 1992
A member of the Namara Group
27/29 Goodge Street, London W1P 1FD

First published in Italian under the title *Teorema* by
Garzanti Editore
Copyright © by Garzanti Editore s.p.a., Milan
1968, 1969, 1991
Translation copyright © by Quartet Books Limited 1992

A catalogue record for this book is available from the
British Library

ISBN 0 7043 0157 1

Printed and bound in Great Britain by
BPCC Hazells Ltd
Member of BPCC Ltd

CONTENTS

INTRODUCTION

In the spring of 1968 Pasolini, whose reputation as a film-maker was already established, shot in Lombardy a film called *Theorem*; before it had reached the screen he had published a novel of the same name. It was, as he explained, as if the book had been painted with one hand while with the other he was working on a fresco – the film. Both works stemmed from an idea that had taken shape some five years before. Both appear to have come to maturity together – in parallel – so that it would be a deep misunderstanding to call the novel 'the book of the film'; which did not prevent some critics of the day from dismissing it as little more than a film treatment.

Both the novel and the film should be seen against the attempt to find a way out of the neo-realist tradition which had dominated Italian writing and film-making in the immediate post-war years – a change of direction that coincided with the realization that, on the one hand, the ideals of the Resistance were not going to be achieved and that, on the other, there was a danger of nostalgic mythologies. So *Theorem* the novel aims at a new objectivity reminiscent of the *nouveau roman*. The meticulous detail distances the characters, their milieu and their actions. The narrative is told in a historical present which denies attempts to set the action at a particular time, season or date. Pasolini, the film-maker, said that what inspired his cinematographic style were the frescoes of Massaccio and Giotto. His lens concentrated on foreground images (in particular the faces of the characters); what surrounded them was conceived of as the background or painting of a stage-set. In *Theorem*, the novel, the same detached eye studies the landscape of Lombardy with its poplars and ditches, the city-scapes with the bourgeois villas and new factories, against which the characters are seen in close-up. The effect is an example of that estrangement defined and described by the Russian formalists. It is an effect to which the organization of the book contributes; for it appears to aim at formal proof (a theorem) with data and corollaries laid out in a manner reminiscent of Spinoza's philosophical method.

The question left unanswered by both the film and the book is: What precisely is the theorem Pasolini is intent on demonstrating? In narrative terms it concerns the consequences of the epiphany of a beautiful young man in the staid family of a Milanese industrialist. One possible reading is that the young man is an X or perhaps better an E (E for Eros), but at all events a demiurge, who has the usual ambivalence of demiurges in that his powers are both positive and negative. His seduction of each member of the household in turn therefore has results at once intense and devastating. The theorem might be stated formally in these terms: E plus the industrialist/his wife/his son/his daughter/the peasant girl who is their maid servant/ equals self-discovery, self-realization, fulfilment. Self-discovery takes place on several planes. Thus the father confronts his homosexuality and at the same time gives his factory to his workers; the wife admits to her sexual needs and realizes the aridity of her social role; the son after his homosexual initiation turns to painting. But the teenage daughter has a harder fate for she is left in a catatonic condition from which (it is suggested) she may not recover. The destiny of the maid is to achieve sainthood and in death to perform miracles. She is the personification of that peasant piety which Pasolini had found so attractive in his youth and childhood among the peasants of Friuli in north-east Italy.

The novel, like the film, bears the imprint of the two forces which tugged against each other in Pasolini's consciousness – the attraction of Christianity (but not of the Church which had denounced him for his sexuality) and that of Marxism (although the Communist Party had been equally condemnatory of his sexual behaviour). It was a dilemma which was by its nature probably incapable of resolution. In the novel, which is naturally more discursive than the film, the narrative is interrupted by long poems which are commentaries on the moral dilemmas of the characters, on the social results of their actions, on capitalism and consumerism. These are meditations expressed in terms of Pauline theology – the father bears the name of the Saint and undergoes a Pauline conversion. To Pasolini, St Paul – about whom he planned a film – was the man who had in a revolutionary manner demolished Roman society, which was founded on class violence, imperialism and slavery; the Roman aristocracy of Paul's day had their parallel in the bourgeoisie of Pasolini's times who would be overthrown by an alliance of progressive bourgeois elements, workers and the subproletarians of the slums.

Perhaps it is Pauline misogyny that informs Pasolini's attitude towards his women characters whose fates on the face of it are more desperate that those of the men – although Pasolini would naturally not accept that sainthood was other than a great blessing. To the present-day reader however his picture of women and their destinies must seem harsh. The maidservant and the daughter are disturbing images of female sacrifice and submission.

The book was entered for the prestigious Strega literary prize but – although Pasolini in his usual way canvassed actively by letter – won only second place, whereupon Pasolini withdrew from the competition amid uproar in literary circles. He then entered the film for the Venice Film Festival but withdrew it there because he disapproved of the policy pursued by the festival director in awarding prizes. Shown to critics outside the festival it caused a scandal because the demiurge (played by Terence Stamp) was shown nude. Awarded a prize by left-wing Catholics it was violently attacked by the Papal authorities. The public prosecutor ordered its confiscation for obscenity but at the trial (one of many similar prosecutions) Pasolini defended his work as an illustration of the effects of the irruption of the divine into everyday life. The verdict was an acquittal. The film was judged to be a poetic work.

This was Pasolini's last fictional work. From now on he would, as Moravia had guessed, turn to film-making as his main narrative medium. In the cinema his oeuvre concluded with the – in the precise sense of the word – terrible and terrifying *Salò or the 120 Days of Sodom*. Here, as in *Theorem*, the theme is once again Eros which St Paul saw as a destructive force, that fire from which men should escape, and which Pasolini saw can be turned into a weapon in the hands of tyrants.

Stuart Hood

Theorem

PART ONE

1

DATA

The first data in this story of ours consist, very modestly, of the description of the life of a family. It concerns a petty bourgeois family – petty bourgeois in the ideological not the economic sense. In fact, the case of many rich people who live in Milan. We think it is not difficult for the reader to imagine how these persons live; how they behave in their relations with their background (which is precisely that of the rich industrial bourgeoisie); how they act in their family circle and so on. We also believe that it is not difficult either (thus permitting us to avoid certain details of dress, which are not new) to imagine these persons one by one; in fact, it is in no way a case of exceptional persons but of persons who are more or less average.

The midday bells are ringing. With the sound of the bells there mix the discreet and almost sweet wails of the hooters.

A factory occupies the whole horizon (which is very indistinct because of the mist which not even the midday light is able to dispel) with its walls of a green as tender as the pale blue of the sky. The season is undefined (it could be spring or the beginning of autumn – or both together because this story does not follow a chronology) and the poplars which, in long regular ranks, ring the immense clearing where (only a few months or years ago) the factory rose, are bare and just beginning to bud (or else have dry leaves).

When midday is announced the workers begin to leave the

factory and the rows of parking places, of which there are hundreds upon hundreds, begin to come alive . . .

It is in these surroundings, against this background, that the first character in our story presents himself.

From the factory's main gate – to the almost military salutes of the porters – a Mercedes slowly emerges: in it, with a sweet and worried face that is a little lifeless, that of a man who all his life has been concerned only with business and, occasionally, with sport, is the owner – or at least the principal shareholder – of that factory. His age is somewhere between forty and fifty: but he is very youthful (his face is tanned and his hair is only slightly grey, his body still agile and muscular, precisely that of someone who played games in his youth and continues to do so). His gaze is lost in the void; it could be worried, bored or simply inexpressive – therefore indecipherable. For him to enter and leave the factory of which he is the boss so solemnly is merely a habit. In short, he has the air of a man deeply immersed in his life: the fact of being an important man on whom the fates of many others depend makes him – as can happen – remote, alien, mysterious. But this is a mystery, so to speak, that is poor in substance and in nuances.

His car leaves behind it in the factory, which is as long as the horizon and almost suspended in the sky, and takes the road to Milan which has just been built through the old poplars.

2

MORE DATA (I)

The midday bells are ringing.

Pietro, the second character in our story – son of the first one – comes out of the door of the *liceo*. (Or perhaps he has already left it and is going home along the everyday streets).

He too, like his father, bears on his brow, which is not high (in fact rather low), the light of an intelligence which is that of someone who has not lived his adolescence in a very rich Milanese family in vain; but – more obviously than the father – he has suffered for it: so that instead of emerging as a boy sure of himself and perhaps keen on sport like his father, what has emerged is a weak boy, with a low, slightly violet brow, with eyes already cowed by hypocrisy, with a lock of hair that is still slightly coxcombish; already deadened by a future as a bourgeois boy whose destiny is not to fight.

Altogether, Pietro is reminiscent of some character from the old silent films, we might actually say – mysteriously and irresistibly – Charlie Chaplin; but to tell the truth without any reason. Yet one cannot help thinking, on seeing him, that he, like Chaplin, is made to wear coats and jackets which are too big for him with sleeves that hang inches beyond his hands – or to run behind a tram he will never catch – or to slip in a dignified way on a banana skin in some grey and tragically solitary district of a city.

These however are merely lively and extempore reflections; the reader must not let himself be distracted by them. For now Pietro can be perfectly well be imagined as any young Milanese *liceo* student, recognized by his companions in every possible way as a brother, one of the gang, a comrade, in their innocent class war, which has just begun and is already so confident.

He is walking along, in fact, with a slily happy air, beside a blonde girl clearly of his class and from the same social tradition, who is undoubtedly, for the time being, his girl. There must not be any doubts about this. Pietro, on his way home, across the fine lawns of a Milanese public park, which are touched by a baking sun (this too is an impalpable possession of someone who owns the city), is *sincerely* taken up with courting his schoolmate. He is doing it, it is true, as if he were following a painful plan: but that is due only to his secret access of shyness, to which he cannot confess, which is masked by a sense of humour and an air of confidence from which, moreover, even if he so wished, he *would not be able* to free himself.

His companions – all correctly dressed, in spite of a certain vague tendency towards the loutish, with faces which, whether touching or antipathetic, are marked by the precocious lack of any kind of unselfishness, of any purity – connive to leave the couple behind. So Pietro and his girl linger joking beside a bush – blonde as ears of wheat (if it is autumn), tenderly transparent (if it is spring); then they go and sit on a secluded bench, they embrace, they kiss; the occasional passing by of detested witnesses (a victim of paralysis, for example who is walking along in the sunlight which to him is merely consolatory) interrupts them in their most guilty gestures (her hand near his lap but a lap that is without violence); but this is their good right and their relationship is after all sincere, nice and free.

3

MORE DATA (II)

The midday bells are ringing.

Odetta, Pietro's sister, who is younger, is also coming home from her school; it is run by an order of nuns. She is very sweet and disturbing, poor Odetta; with a brow that looks like a small box full of painful intelligence, indeed almost of *wisdom*.

Like the children of the poor who are suddenly adult and already know everything about life, sometimes the children of the rich are also precocious – old with the age of their class: so they live, as if it were a kind of illness, by a kind of unwritten code instinctively known by heart – but with a sense of humour comparable to the sweet happiness of poor children.

Odetta seems to be principally intent on hiding all this – an effort which is not however crowned with success, because it is precisely this visible effort that betrays her true soul. If her face is oval and beautiful (with a few conventionally poetical freckles), her eyes big, with long lashes and her nose short and precise, her mouth, on the other hand, is an almost embarrassing revelation of what Odetta really is: not that it is ugly, that mouth, indeed it is extremely pretty – and yet it is slightly monstrous, that's the truth; it is so pronounced and distinctive that one cannot fail to notice it for an instant with that receding lower lip like those in the mouths of baby rabbits or mice: what we are talking about, in substance, is the odd twist of a sense of humour – or else the painful, masked consciousness of one's nullity – without which Odetta's sense of humour could not live.

So, now, as she walks along at the same time as her brother Pietro, Odetta has all the external and common characteristics of a very rich young girl who is allowed by her family (because of a certain snobbery) to dress and behave in a modern kind of way (in spite of the nuns).

Odetta also has a boy who courts her – a soft, tall idol of his social class and race. Round them too, there is a group of comrades, barely adolescent boys and girls, who already behave entirely naturally according to the latest style – unsuspecting, perfect reproductions of their parents.

The talk between Odetta and her callow suitor turns on an album of photographs which Odetta is clasping jealously along with her school books. An album with a little velvet cover full of pink and red squiggles in the Liberty style. This album is still completely empty – evidently just bought at a stationer's. Only the first page has been inaugurated with a large photograph – a photograph of her father.

Her suitor is joking a little about this album as if he were fully aware that it is an old craze of the girl's; but when he becomes a little bolder, a single gesture, a single word – near a fountain of dark stone, under rows of small trees that seem to be of metal – Odetta runs off.

Here is an elegant and capricious flight, entirely devoid of expression, but which in reality hides real terror. And what she says among her young friends, both boys and girls, to her suitor who pursues her excitedly – 'I don't like men' – is said with arrogance and an elegant sense of humour: yet it is clear that, somehow or other, it conceals a certain truth.

4

MORE DATA (III)

As the reader will already have noticed, this, rather than being a story, is what in the sciences is called 'a report': so it is full of information; therefore, technically, its shape rather than being that of 'a message', is that of 'a code'. Moreover it is not realistic but, on the contrary, is emblematic – enigmatic – so that any preliminary information about the identity of the characters has a purely indicative value – it serves the concreteness not the substance of things.

The reader can imagine Lucia, the mother of Pietro and Odetta, in a calm and secret corner of the house – a bedroom or *boudoir* or little drawing-room or veranda – with timid reflections of the green of the garden and so on. But Lucia is not there as the guardian angel of the house – no, she is there as a bored woman. She has found a book, has begun to read it and now her reading absorbs her (it is a rare and intelligent book on the life of animals). In this way she is waiting for dinner-time. As she reads, a lock of hair falls over one eye (an expensive lock produced by a hairdresser perhaps in the course of this same morning). As she leans forward she exposes her cheekbones to the radiant light, they are high and as if vaguely consumed and funereal – with a certain invalid flush. Her eyes, instantly lowered, seem long, black, vaguely cyanotic and barbaric, perhaps because of their dark liquid quality.

But when she moves, raising her eyes from the book for a moment to look at the time on her little wristwatch (to do so she must raise her arm and expose it more to the light), for an instant one has the impression (fleeting and perhaps basically false) that she looks like a girl from the people.

However that may be, her fate as a sedentary person, her cult of beauty (which in her is more of a function – one that is her due in a division of powers), the obligation to have an enlightened intelligence against a background that remains instinctively reactionary, has perhaps gradually made her rigid, has made her too a little mysterious, like her husband. And if in her, too, this mystery is a somewhat lacking in depth and lights and shades, it is nevertheless much more sacred and immobile (although behind it a fragile Lucia is perhaps struggling, the child of times that were economically less happy).

Let us add that when Emilia, the maid, comes to say that the meal is served (disappearing at once, sullenly, through the doorway) Lucia, after rising lazily and throwing the book lazily into the least suitable spot – perhaps simply letting it fall to the ground – quickly and almost absent-mindedly makes the sign of the cross.

5

MORE DATA (IV)

This scene, too, and the following one in the story, the reader must read only as providing hints. So the description is not meticulous and worked out in detail as in any traditional or simply normal story. We repeat, this is not a realistic story, it is a parable; and moreover we have not yet penetrated to the heart of events, we are still at the stage of statements.

Taking advantage of that beautiful sun, the family is lunching in the open air; the children have just got back from school, their father from the factory – now they are all gathered round the table. The residential district affords them the peace of the countryside. The garden surrounds the whole house. The table has been placed in a space in the sun far from the bushes and the clumps of trees whose shade is still a little cool.

Beyond the garden is the street or rather a wide avenue – a suburban one but the kind you get in residential suburbs – which can just be seen with the roofs of other houses and blocks of flats, which are elegant and rigidly silent.

The family is lunching in seclusion, and Emilia serves them. Emilia is an ageless girl, who could as easily be eight as thirty-eight – a poor girl from the Italian north – one who is excluded from the white race. (It is very probable that she comes from some village in the plains not far from Milan and yet still entirely peasant, perhaps from round Lodi itself, from the places which gave birth to a saint who probably resembled her, Saint Maria Cabrini).

11

The bell rings.

Emilia runs to open the door and what appears before her eyes is Angiolino,[1] the person we can consider to be the seventh character in our story, or to put it better, a kind of joker. Everything about him in fact has a magical air – his absurdly thick curls, which fall down over his eyes like a poodle's, his funny face covered with pimples and his crescent-shaped eyes, charged with an endless reserve of mirth. This is the postman. And he is there with a telegram in his hand, in front of Emilia, who is his equal but who nevertheless *has no opinion of him*. But instead of giving her the telegram he interrogates her, his face lit up by an over-flowing sweet smile, winking at her and pointing with his head towards the garden where the master and mistress are eating. Then abandoning Emilia, who is shut off behind her barrier of silence, he runs to the corner of the villa and from there looks secretively towards the people who are carrying out the lunchtime ritual of the rich, looking for Odetta (whom he courts out of pure heedlessness). Finally, for-getting Odetta and everything else with the same speed as he had remembered them, he goes back to being Emilia's accomplice and after smirking merrily at her a couple of times (he includes her in his courtship of Odetta) he finally hands the telegram over to her – and goes off, running with comical haste but without anxiety towards the gate.

Emilia takes the telegram to the family which continues to eat silently in the sun. The father raises his eyes from the bourgeois newspaper he is reading and opens the telegram in which is written: 'I SHALL ARRIVE TOMORROW' (the father's thumb covers the name of the signatory). Evidently everyone

[1]Angiolo or Angiolino is, as his name implies, the announcing angel – the messenger (Tr.).

had been waiting for this telegram and their curiosity had therefore already passed before its confirmation: so they continue indifferently with their lunch in the open air.

6

END OF EXPOSITION

The interior of our family's house is all lit up although it is tea-time and the long sunset is still sending out its light, laden with the silence of the slim poplars and of the lawns, flat and green, swollen with water. Since it is probably Sunday they are giving a little party, the guests being almost all young people – or else school-friends of Pietro and Odetta.

But there are also ladies, the mothers of these young people. In the confusion (which in these cases has always an elegiac air, because the people there lose the miserable and often hateful weight of their persons and crumble in the sweetness of the atmosphere – of that atmosphere which is made up of electric light and sunlight coming from the plain) the new and extraordinary character in our story now makes his appearance.

Extraordinary because of his beauty – a beauty so exceptional as to have the effect of being in scandalous contrast to all the others present. Even if one watched him carefully, in fact, one would say that he is a foreigner, not only because of his height and the blue of his eyes but because he is so completely devoid of mediocrity, of recognizable qualities and of vulgarity, so that he could not even be thought of as a boy from an Italian petty bourgeois family. Nor could one, on the other hand, say that he has the innocent sensuality and the grace of a boy from the people . . . He is in short socially mysterious, although he fits in perfectly with

14

all the others standing round him in that drawing-room which is magically lit up by the sun.

His presence, therefore, in that absolutely normal party is almost scandalous – but scandalous in a way that is still pleasant and charged with benevolent suspense. His diversity consists basically only in his beauty. And everyone, the ladies and the girls, look at him – naturally without showing it too much, everyone knowing very well within themselves the principal rule of the game, which consists in never revealing oneself, at any cost.

So within the limits of the most casual discretion, some friend of Odetta's or some young friend of her mother's asks who that beautiful new boy is. But Odetta shrugs. And Lucia confines herself to some scraps of information which are equally casual. If not to a pure and simple smile. In short we shall not know anything about him; in any case it is not necessary to know. So we shall leave incomplete and in suspension this last item in our exposition.

7

THE SACRED SEX OF THE GUEST

It is an afternoon in late spring (or, given the ambiguous nature of our story, of early autumn), a silent afternoon. The noises of the city – they are very distant – can scarcely be heard.

A slanting sun lights up the garden. The house is strangely silent; probably everyone is out. In the garden only the young guest has remained. He is sitting in a deck chair or on a wicker couch. He is reading with his head in the shade and his body in the sun.

As we shall see better shortly from the details of his body in the sun – when, following the glances that watch him, we are close to him – he is reading textbooks on medicine or engineering.

The silence of the garden in the profound peace of that uninvolved and consoling sun, with the first geraniums beginning to blossom (or else with the first pomegranate leaves falling), is broken by an irritating, monotonous and excessive noise: it is that of a little lawnmower which squeaks as it moves up and down the lawn, starting up its confused din in the same way each time, without interruption.

It is Emilia who is pushing the lawnmower up and down in that way.

She is in a corner of the garden at the far end of a smooth, flat lawn of a dark green that is almost blinding, while the youth is in another corner, near the house under an ivy-covered pergola.

Every so often, the obsessive noise of the mower is interrupted; and Emilia stops, upright for a few moments. She gazes towards the youth in a very strange way like someone who does not have the courage to look and at the same time is so unaware that she feels no shame at her own insistence. On the contrary, her gaze becomes almost veiled as if she were the one who was offended by that indiscreet insistence.

How long does Emilia continue to go up and down with the mower, stopping and looking, then starting to go up and down again, stooping and sweating? And how long, unaware, not only of her but also of the fact that he is paying no attention to her, does the youth continue to read his textbooks. For a long time, perhaps all morning – or else for the short morning the day has in rich houses where ten o'clock is a time almost before dawn. The sun rises further in the clear sky until it becomes scorching – in an arid summer peace.

Emilia continues to push the mower, madly, clumsily (besides this should not even be her business but the gardener's. She has long since taken over responsibility for the lawn because of a kind of rivalry with the gardener himself since she is the daughter of peasants and comes straight from the countryside).

So the youth does not notice that he is being watched, for he is completely and almost innocently immersed in his studies – which in Emilia's eyes is an almost sacred privilege. All the more so since now – perhaps in order to rest a little – instead of the textbooks he is reading a slim volume of Rimbaud's poetry in a cheap edition. And this absorbs him even more than his previous reading.

At first the servant's glance, when she stops to look at him, is a rapid and fleeting one which can therefore take in only the guest's whole figure with his head in the shade and his body in the sun.

But then her glance becomes sharper and lingers longer on that distant object which does not react; while her forearm is passed over her brow to dry the sweat, she sullenly explores the details of that body which offers itself to her down there so completely and unconsciously.

Very slowly, in this way, her gestures – which seem obsessive only because they have something mechanically simple about them – becomes obsessive in an explicit and almost ostentatious manner.

That is to say that walking up and down performing the humble task of cutting the grass loses its naturalness, its quality of an everyday chore and becomes almost the external form of an obscure intent.

In fact, the way she continually looks at the guest comes to have about it a hint of suspicion and madness. So much so that finally – as if she could no longer resist (but the guest still does not notice, being immersed in his reading and, besides, being socially and intellectually so distant form her) – Emilia in a theatrical manner leaves the mower in the middle of the lawn and almost runs into the house.

She passes through the living-room, the kitchen and goes into her little room, as small as a cell and in it such luxuries as the owners allow her and her own poor gaudy things. Here she begins to carry out actions which might seem normal but, in reality, because of the frenzied and inopportune way in which they are done, seem absurd. She combs her hair. She takes out her earrings. She prays (a short prayer, half conventionally devout and half ecstatic), then she recovers herself after kissing a holy picture with the Sacred Heart over and over again and goes out. Still in a theatrical way, she goes back to her mower.

Now her obsessive ceremonial starts again, up and down with the mower over the grass, always with a troubled and innocent gaze that explores the youth's body.

Little by little the contemplation of that body becomes unbearable. And she rebels in a rage against her own temptation.

She runs off again but this time in a still more clamorous way – that is to say weeping and almost shouting as if overcome by an attack of hysteria.

She tramples the grass in the garden like a mad sheep and gasping for breath, goes back into the house.

She goes through the living-room once more, rushes into the kitchen, and with a violent gesture – but one that is slightly dream-like and idiotic – detaches the gas-pipe as if she really meant to kill herself.

This time the youth had perforce to notice her, take an interest in her. He cannot but have heard that weeping and those mad sobs, he cannot but have glimpsed the woman's flight, which clearly demanded to be seen and noted by him. So he follows her, almost running like her, and catches up with her in the kitchen. Here he naturally sees her making those mad gestures of protest of hers. He comes to her help. He tears the gas pipe from her hands, tries to revive her, to comfort her, to find a way of interrupting that rush of pain which no longer recognizes anything.

He drags her into her little room and lays her on the bed – lays her down, while Emilia is already beginning to toss about and gasp less wildly and to show a wish to be calmed and consoled.

In all this – as he lifts her up, as he talks to her, as he lays her on that sad bed – the young guest has a strangely protective air that is almost maternal; like a mother who knew her child's whims and anticipated them with a kind of loving awareness.

19

There is also a fine thread of irony in the way he deals with her, in his unsurprised patience. It is as if the woman's madness, her weakness, the sudden collapse of all resistance and therefore of any dignity – the collapse of the whole world of duties – awoke in him merely a kind of loving compassion, precisely of delicate maternal caring.

This attitude of his and the expression in his eyes, which seemed to say, 'It's nothing serious!' became still more marked when Emilia (flattered by his acts of tenderness and his caresses – and blindly obedient to her instinct, which now was unrestrained) almost mechanically, with a kind of inspiration more mystical than hysterical, pulled her skirt up above her knees.

This seems to be the only way she has – without awareness and without words or, by now, without shame – of declaring herself, of offering the boy something as a supplicant. And precisely because it is tremendous it also has a certain purity and an animalistic humility.

Then the boy – still with a protective maternal air that is sweetly ironical – pulls down her skirt a little as if to defend that shame she has forgotten and which on the contrary is everything to her. Then he caresses her face.

Emilia weeps from shame – even though it is not a case of that special kind of weeping which is the outburst that comes, in a childish way, when the crisis is already subsiding, consoled.

He dries her tears with his fingers.

She kisses the fingers that are caressing her with the respect and humility of a dog or of a daughter kissing her father's hands.

Nothing stands in the way of their love and the youth lays himself on top of the woman's body, accepting her desire to be possessed by him.

8

THE DEGRADING MISERY OF ONE'S OWN NAKED BODY AND THE REVEALING POWER OF THE NAKED BODY OF ONE'S COMPANION

In the little white road in the middle of the villa's green lawn, near the gate, light and elegant people are arriving: a lady of Lucia's age, some girls, perhaps her daughters and so many suitcases and bags, all of dark, precious kinds of leather. The murky air on which a sun is shining, perhaps filtered by distant mist, gives to their arrival a floating and unreal air; which is contradicted however by the naïve cries and the exaggerated displays of joy which even rich and well-educated people permit themselves on certain occasions. To receive these suitcase-laden guests there are Lucia (who is almost skeletal in her severe elegance) and her children. They all go in, out of the troubled air outside with that excessively green lawn, into the air inside which is well shielded by the little gleaming windows of the villa.

The result of this arrival is that after a while – or in the evening – Emilia, bent double by the weight of a big (man's) suitcase comes into Pietro's bedroom. Here she puts the suitcase down (with respectful delicacy because it is a guest's) and devotedly goes away.

So the guest and the son sleep in the same bedroom. It is evening, we go in along with them.

Pietro's room is that of a boy who is beginning to turn into a young man. It still has some of the fantastic characteristics of the bedroom of a firstborn middle-class son (it is furnished, that is to say, with the taste their mothers attribute to their own sons so that they become modern through them and the nest for childish dreams becomes a display of fauve painters, of comic strips and American heroes for childhood). At the same time, however, the room – changing with the son's age – is no longer that of a child but that of a youth superimposed on the other, just as two different styles are superimposed on the façade of the same church. The new style is very spare and elegant, without anything superfluous, even if two or three pieces of furniture are antique.

Naturally, there are two beds: one is a proper brass bed, elegant and probably chosen by the mother; but the other is a divan-bed, it, too, naturally very elegant (in fact a little too elegant because of the need to be camouflaged).

Then the two boys, the young man and the youth, go to bed at the same time, taciturn and perhaps a little tired.

(Is this evening before or after the day in which the incident with Emilia took place? It can be before or after it, that is not important).

So the two go into the bedroom. Perhaps it is late, perhaps they are sleepy or perhaps the silence is due – and this is the most probable hypothesis – to the sense of shame they experience – not without a strange and unpleasant feeling on Pietro's part – when they enter the bedroom together and undress there to go to bed.

In fact while the young guest – perhaps more experienced and, in short, more adult – moves with a certain ease, the other seems embarrassed and hampered in his movements by something which makes him excessively concentrated, bored, stiff. The young guest undresses as is natural in front of the boy – to the point of remaining completely naked without any fear, without any particular sense of shame, as happens – or should happen – in the majority of cases between young people of the same sex and of about the same age.

Pietro, we repeat, visibly feels a deep and unnatural sense of shame which might even be explicable (since he is the smaller) and could even be the source of greater grace in him, if it were taken with a pinch of humour and a touch of anger. Instead Pietro is made surly by it. His pallor becomes more wan, the seriousness of his brown eyes turns mean and a little miserable.

To undress and get into his pyjamas he lies down under the sheets, executing with great difficulty that operation which is so easy.

The young guest – full of that serenity of his which, however, does not harm anyone who lacks it – falls asleep, into that mysterious sleep of healthy persons. Pietro is unable to fall asleep; he remains with open eyes, he turns over under the sheets – he does everything which anyone does who suffers from stupid insomnia as humiliating as an unjust punishment.

9

RESISTANCE TO REVELATION

Does some time pass?

In the heart of the night Pietro is still awake, still in the grip of the thought he has that will not let him sleep and which he himself is probably unable to decipher.

Suddenly he gets up. Very quietly, for fear that the guest may waken, indeed terrified by the idea, pale with anxiety and trembling with fear of being caught in the act, he takes a few steps through the room, approaches the guest and takes a long look at his face, his arms, his naked chest. He contemplates that tranquil sleep, virile and warm. He remains thus, lost and far away, in that state of contemplation.

10

THE YOUNG ANGEL – COMES AND GOES

In the garden the young guest, Lucia and Odetta are seated round a table on which a white table-cloth ripples with flowers, long and white or slightly orange.

The garden, which is very large, with its English-style lawns, the entrance to the house and the street further down are on the same plane, a single setting at the same height.

In front of the garden as far as the eye can see, to the left, there stretches the last misty outskirts with factory walls as white and as diaphanous as gauze and, to the right, the street with its villas and its hard, oblique, silent blocks of flats.

All around there is a silent peace in which, however, there are sounds full of life and of profound, intimate sweetness.

Into this silent midday rest, which the guest shares with Lucia and Odetta, who do not talk, do not exchange anything but banal words which have other meanings that are obscure and perhaps inexpressible, there enters unexpectedly, performing a kind of solo turn – it is slightly absurd and certainly arbitrary – the postboy with his curls, half innocent, half impudent, as if miraculously sent from the distant city. He comes bringing the afternoon post made up entirely of unsealed envelopes and printed matter, which no one is expecting and no one opens.

He comes from the direction of the avenue with its hazy conifers, enters by the garden gate and comes in, appearing and disappearing behind the hedge, then enters the door of the villa.

It is well known in the house that he pays a kind of court to Odetta – an innocent court, paid for the sake of paying it, by instinct, by magic: everyone knows this and everyone is amused; it is a little afternoon tradition.

His laughing, crescent-shaped eyes find their way through the sparse leaves (because they are eaten away by autumn or because still in bud) and they communicate pure and simple happiness.

Now he presents himself at the door, rings, makes some silent remark to Emilia, who entirely disapproves of him and has come out to receive him in a bad temper with downcast eyes – and then goes off singing, forgetting even to look towards Odetta as if he were attracted only by the sun of everyday existence which shines bright on the distant city.

11

THE DEFINITION OF ONESELF AS
THE INSTRUMENT OF SCANDAL

Perhaps it is still the same night as when we left Pietro
contemplating the sleeping guest. (We underline it for the
last time – the facts of this story are as one in place and time.)

Pietro is now stretched out on the bed but he is not yet
sleeping. He is kept awake by his feverish thought. He is a
man who is fighting – he is trying to explain to himself what
is overwhelming him with such unexpected brutality.

Suddenly, almost brusquely, he gets up, drawn by the
mysterious power which has been born within him this night.
He gets up, or rather gets up once again. And, trembling, he
once more approaches the bed in which the guest is sleeping.

We have already said this: Pietro has all the characteristics
of bourgeois psychology and bourgeois beauty. He is rather
pale, and it is as if his good health is due to the fact that he
leads a very clean and healthy life, does gymnastics and plays
a sport. But that pallor has something hereditary about it – or
rather, something impersonal. Something else – humanity,
the world, his social class – is pale in him.

His eyes are very intelligent – but this is an intelligence
rendered impure as it were by an intellectual sickness, of
which he is certainly unaware, for he makes up for it by the
confidence his birth offers him in his way of understanding
things, of acting.

There is therefore an initial obstacle which inevitably
prevents him from understanding and, above all, from

admitting what is happening to him. In order to be able to use his intelligence – really or realistically – he would have to be entirely remade from the beginning. His social class lives its true life in him. So it is not by understanding or admitting things but only by acting that he will be able to grasp the reality of which his bourgeois reason deprives him; only by acting as if in a dream, or better, acting before deciding.

Now he is there trembling by the guest's bed. And precisely as if obeying an impulse stronger than himself (but which comes from within him) – the same impulse as made him leave the bed – he carries out an act which up to a few moments before he would not even have dreamt of being able to carry out or rather to wish to carry out.

Very slowly, he pulls down the light cover lying on the guest's naked body, making it slip along his limbs. His hand is trembling, what is almost a groan comes from his throat.

But at that gesture, which uncovers him down to the belly, the guest suddenly wakes up. He looks at the boy bent over him, who is doing something so absurd to him, and suddenly his eyes fill with that light which we know already in him – that paternal light that is full of maternal closeness which is both understanding and sweetly ironical.

Pietro raises his eyes from the belly, which is uncovered down to the first hair of the loins, and encounters that look. He does not have time to understand it; shame and terror blind him. Weeping and hiding his face he goes and throws himself on his bed and hides with his head in the pillow.

Then the guest gets up and goes and sits on the edge of Pietro's bed: he is motionless for a little looking at the back of that neck shaken by sobs, then – with the comradeship of someone of the same age – he caresses it.

12

MERELY A CASE OF ADULTERY?

The guest is down there, far off, alone, among the waterside plants, against the patches of coppiced wood which have just come into bud.

But there is already the heat of a spring that is far advanced; and now what comes to mind are the profound silences and burning, pleasant afternoon hours of summer. There come to mind too, afternoons long ago, of past centuries (a bell, scarcely noticeable but clear, rings midday); the branches – still dry or just veined by the green of the first tiny leaves – are almost rust- or blood-coloured or sad yellow, it is true, but one feels that they are that nature which is not represented but imagined behind the stone scenes on the Romanesque baptisteries, massive and powerful depictions of a daily life lived along the tributaries of the Po and, precisely, warmed by a similar sun and surrounded by similar fragile and milk-shaped thickets.

The young guest is half-naked – he is running, playing with a friendly dog along the bank of a pond of some sort, which is intensely green: an ox-bow on the course of the Ticino. He is in a festive mood, as strong and happy as a boy as he runs to and fro or throws himself into the water with a cane in his hand, which makes his friend the dog go mad with joy.

Watching the guest playing down there at the bottom of a steep slope which faces the wood is Lucia. She is sitting on the top of some kind of embankment and has behind her a sunny meadow at the far end of which, raised on elegant piles, a large chalet rises. For a long time from up there – very far from any stranger's eyes because of the luxurious wildness of the spot – Lucia stays watching the boy playing; she is expressionless. Expressionless like someone who within herself is making difficult calculations but ones which, to judge by a certain light in her eyes, are about to be solved. The result of these calculations for the time being is that she crosses the meadow and slowly goes into the chalet.

There, in the half-light, she looks carefully around her. There is a little alcove divided off by a big curtain. This rich Milanese family wanted to have here, in this spot, an almost empty house: an elegant space in which to camp almost in discomfort. The curtain is open and one sees in a corner a bed with big dark blankets. On the dark blankets the boy's clothes – summer clothes, almost all brightly coloured – stand out in the light reflected through the shutters.

Lucia stands looking at them for a long time with, in her eyes, that rapid and complicated thought-process which has her entirely in its grasp – as it did before when faced by the boy playing in the copse.

Then, very very slowly, calmly and with that particular light in her eyes which seems to be merely the final and positive result of a tranquil calculation, she approaches the clothes which gleam almost violently, scattered on the bed. She crouches down, kneels before them.

There is the youth's jersey or shirt, his T-shirt; there are his shoes, his watch, his underpants, his socks.

Lucia looks at them.

The clothes are there, innocent under her gaze, as if abandoned.

It is easy to examine them because they offer no resistance;

30

indeed they offer themselves with excessive and unprotected humility.

The underpants are rolled up into a ball like a rag; the socks lie apart from each other as if worn by a man with his legs open but sleeping deeply; the T-shirt is of an almost unnatural white, too pure. In short these clothes are like the relics of someone who has gone away for ever.

Perhaps it is at this thought – 'He has gone away for ever and his clothes are left behind here to bear witness to him' – that Lucia feels a pang in her heart and she does not restrain the gesture with which she represses it or the expression of pain which contracts her mouth like a kind of nostalgia – nostalgia for something lost without even having been had.

Or perhaps her insistent contemplation of these insignificant objects is a kind of revelation to her. Through which she understands suddenly who he really is – now that he is not there – this person who uses them, who warmed them with the natural warmth of his body and now seems to have abandoned them there unintentionally to bear witness to him.

Very slowly Lucia's eyes lose their look of contemplative indifference and are filled with tenderness. Those, it is true, are the clothes of a youth who could be her son – so the tenderness they awaken in her is a kind of maternal fetishism.

She takes them up, looks at them and perhaps caresses them; her hand also passes in a shamelessly natural way over those parts of the clothes over which they could never pass when they were being worn. She repeats this gesture frequently, without losing her dignity, like a mother tending the wounds of her son. But these gestures, being repeated, slowly take her out of herself. Now she is like Pietro, possessed by a dream born within her, without being understood or admitted to. *To realize it she too must therefore act*

31

before making a decision. Again, she goes out of the door. Again, she looks at the boy running about down there among the branches which, because there is too much light, have lost all colour.

In the midday silence she hears loudly the joyful barking of Barbin, the dog.

The woman looks at the distant boy and her glance becomes more and more perplexed: now it is as if it is no longer a calculation that swirls within her but something like a prayer. Like an automaton she turns on her heel, climbs the external stair and reaches the little terrace above the chalet. Here she stretches herself out – on the floor of dark wood – as she is certainly accustomed to do every day, but she is unable to lie there crushed between the naked floor and the impossible sky. She gets up again, onto her knees; she leans over the parapet, again looking down through the coppice towards the boy.

He is still there, unattainable, playing, swimming, running through the tree trunks and the bushes.

Then Lucia slowly slips off her costume and remains naked on the terrace behind the low parapet. To remain naked up there in anticipation of sunbathing is probably an everyday habit of hers. So, naked, she continues to watch the boy who still does not notice, being dazed by running in the blinding light.

Until the moment comes when he is tired of his games and his swimming and moves towards the chalet but very slowly, still playing with dog. It is clear that he intends to come in and be with her again – talking or each reading their own book.

With a rapid almost rude gesture Lucia then grabs her costume as if to put it on. But then that particular light that goes with a calculation scarcely guessed at comes back into her eyes, which are staring at the little red bricks of the terrace: the decision to remain naked and to show herself to him naked was already taken – with the same almost hysterical candour and the assent of an unfeeling animal which had been dominant in the resolve of Emilia or of Pietro some days before (or later).

Naturally, unlike Emilia, she struggles against that resolve: modesty and shame – which her social class lives through her – are about to re-establish their natural ascendancy: so she has to fight against that modesty and shame. And once again to overcome the obstacles of her upbringing and her world she has to act before understanding.

Suddenly, she grips her costume, gets up and throws it down, over the parapet of the terrace, to the other side of the pond towards the thickets. She looks at it down there among the grass and blackberry bushes, irretrievable: that it is there is profoundly significant, its loss and its inertia have the expressive violence of objects in dreams.

Now Lucia is naked: *she has forced herself to be so.* She can have no second thoughts. She turns round; the boy is now on the ground below the chalet which is strewn with tufts of grass. She sees him. She sees him go into the chalet and then sees him come out again, look round, call her.

Like a martyr, scarcely rising above the parapet Lucia calls, 'I am here!' He turns, smiles to her with all the innocence and normality of his youth, and nimbly he climbs the stairs that lead to the terrace. Thus he appears against the sky with his eyes looking at her at once.

For an instant Lucia returns that look, which she has invoked, wished for; but not for more than an instant.

The mechanism she herself has set in motion allows her to feel ashamed in his presence. She runs and crouches against the parapet, hiding her loins with her knees and her breasts with her arms.

The pleasure of causing herself to be violated by that look, of having voluntarily lost and degraded himself, coincides with a feeling of shame that may be casual and legitimate: that of having been caught by surprise while she innocently sunbathed on the terrace. She plays this part as diligently and tenaciously as a child; but she consciously plays it badly. She has in fact realized that if she shows excessive, true shame – that of an innocent taken by surprise – the guest might turn that glance which is so divinely degrading away from her and perhaps go off with an apology. So to the true shame she feels – and which is chilling her – and to the false shame she feigns, she must add, as best she can, a coquetry which quickly takes on the almost tearful clumsiness and the troubled shameless-ness of an invitation; a ridiculously wicked smile in her bewildered eyes which quickly give up all pretence and are desperately fixed on the young man.

But he gives that natural glance of his, which is under-standing, perhaps just tinged with a little irony and along with that a great, sweet, protective parent's strength. He approaches her as she presses herself closer and closer to the parapet, hiding herself and holding her head down. He leans over her and strokes her hair and under that caress Lucia dares to raise her eyes to him, filled with a desperately begging look.

13

WHERE THE INITIATION OF A
MIDDLE-CLASS BOY BEGINS

In Pietro's room the young guest, sitting beside Pietro, is turning the pages of a large book of colour prints shining brightly in the afternoon sun that beats down powerfully on the patinaed pages. Pietro is looking at these colour reproductions of a painting he does not know and which up to now – perhaps under the influence of his art history teacher at the *liceo* – he maybe had not known about or did not approve of. (In fact there is in his eyes the attention of one who, almost with gratitude, is discovering something after an initial feeling of distrust).

The picture which the two boys have before them is strongly coloured – with pure colours: if one looks at it more closely it is like a network of outlines which leave free surfaces, triangles and rectangles that are slightly rounded (that is to say as if they were stretched on a curved surface); and it is on these free surfaces that those pure colours are applied: Prussian blue and reds – pure but extremely discreet, almost stealthy, as if veiled by a patina of age. The drawing paper on which these watercolours or tempera paintings are applied – but with the richness and depth of oils – has actually turned yellow; turned a poor yellow; you almost seem to catch the smell of age, of mustiness, of the library. Although it is so absurd, free, fiery, the picture is profoundly severe and its pure colours are not those of Les Fauves. What picture is it? The date is certainly somewhere between 1910 and 1920.

It does not belong to the culture of Cubism, that sumptuous culture. It is spare, extremely spare. Perhaps it is Futurism – but certainly not that dynamic and sensuous Italian brand. Something naïve and popular or infantile might make one think of Russian Futurism, of some minor painter – a friend of Eisenstein, of Shklovsky or of Jakobson, who was active between Moscow and Petersburg or perhaps in Prague as a Cubist. No, here is the signature – Lewis, a friend of Pound, an American of the years of Imagism. A drawing with coloured surfaces, constructed like a perfect machine and so rigorous as to have reduced the picture to the bare bones.

Almost together, Pietro and the young guest lift their eyes from the reproduction of the painting and look at each other – in that mysterious closeness born in the night . . .

But their solitude is interrupted by voices calling from outside – the fresh, youthful and slightly vulgar voices of boys.

Pietro and the guest disengage themselves from the heat of their bodies sitting one beside the other with, on their knees, the book that was their go-between[1] and go out into the garden. They look out from the parapet that gives on to the street and see a group of Pietro's friends and schoolmates. 'Here we are, we're coming,' they shout, and go off almost running through the garden to meet them at the gate.

[1]The whole episode is a reference to the story of Paolo and Francesca in Dante's *Inferno* where the book the lovers were reading before they lifted their eyes and kissed is called a 'go-between' (Tr.).

14

RE-EDUCATION TO DISORDER
AND DISOBEDIENCE

The two boys, Pietro and the guest, along with the other boys, Pietro's school friends (models of *liceo* life) are playing with a ball on a football pitch. In the air there is the utmost Lombard limpidity (not to mention the sound of old bells of the towns or the villages of the north). Life seems to have no hitches, no obstacles, nothing, no unpleasantness. It slips by in that clear light like oil. It is young Pietro's life.

As if seized by an unconsciouus euphoria he and his friends are playing heedlessly round a goal. The joy is that of the game as a game; even those who have no gifts as players enjoy certain easy skills, with which they pass that morning of their youth.

As happens sometimes, Pietro, coming from such a rich family, has not had the money necessary to fit himself out in the best way for playing football: he is wearing the shorts and jersey which people buy in ordinary shops and the football boots (this must be a tradition with him) hurt him because of some nails sticking through the soles. So in the end, limping and rather against his will, he runs to the side of the field to take off his boot and examine it. But when he is there on that clean grass, surrounded by the running-track, by the white and immaculate walls and, further off, by the grey amphitheatre of the outskirts, he is overcome by a kind of bliss. Neither his glance nor life meet any resistance there. He

37

stretches himself out belly up: and very quickly that moment of peace becomes solitude and alienation.

The guest also leaves the group of players – with youthful faces that are already old – and goes and sits beside Pietro. Thus with the pleasure of repeating the same things a hundred times over, proud of their own rebellion against any tradition and filled with a passion at once clean and deep – *which one has only once in one's life* – the two friends begin to talk about literature and painting once more.

15

'THE FIRST ONES WE LOVE ARE ...'

'The first ones we love
are the poets and painters of the previous generation
of the beginning of the century; they assume
in our mind the place of our fathers, remaining
young, however, as in their yellowed photographs.
Poets and painters for whom to be bourgeois was not
  shameful ...
youths in vicuna or felt ...
or poor neckties which told of rebellion and of mothers.
Poets and painters who would become famous
towards the mid-century
with some unknown friends of great value
but, perhaps, out of fear, not suited to poetry
(true poets untimely dead).
Pavements of Vienna or Viareggio! Riverside streets
of Florence or Paris!
Made to ring by those feet of youths
shod with thick boots.
The wind of disobedience smells of cyclamen
over the cities at the feet of the young poets!
The young poets who chatter
after a cheap draught of beer
like bourgeois, independents –
locomotives abandoned but still with fires lit,
forced for a time, onto blind branchlines
to enjoy youth's lack of haste;

certain of being able to change the rotten world
with four impassioned words and a rebel's gait.
The mothers like mother birds
in the little bourgeois houses
entwine the jasmine of the air
with the meaning of a family's private light
and of its place in a nation full of rejoicings.
So the nights re-echo only from the footsteps of the
    youths.
Melancholy has infinite lairs,
infinite like the stars,
in Milan or in another city,
from which to send up its air gently from lit stoves.
The pavements run past eighteenth-century houses;
peeling houses with sacrosanct destinies
(streets of a village that became an industrial city)
with a distant romantic odour of frozen cowsheds.
It is thus that the boy poets experience life.
And what they have to say to each other is what the others
    say,
the non-poet boys (they too, lords of life
and of innocence),
with mothers who sing
at the little windows of inner courtyards
(wells that stink to the unseen stars).
Where have these footsteps vanished to?
A severe little page of memories is not enough
no, it is not enough – perhaps only the poet who was no
    poet
or the painter who was no painter,
dead before or after a war, in some city
of legendary changes of abode
keeps these nights in himself truthfully.

Ah, those footsteps of the youths
from the best families in the city (those
who follow the destiny of the nation
as a horde of animals follows the scent –
aloe, nutmeg, beetroot, cyclamen –
as it migrates) those poets' footsteps
with their painter-friends who tramp the pavements,
talking, talking . . .
But if this is the scheme of things, the truth is different.
Young men, reproduce those young men.
Do feel nostalgia for them when you are sixteen.
But begin to understand immediately
that the poets and painters old or dead
in spite of the halo of a heroic air you give them
are useless to you, teach you nothing.
Enjoy your first naïve and stubborn experiences,
timid dynamiter, master of the free nights,
but remember you are here only to be hated,
to upset things and to kill.

16

IT IS THE FATHER'S TURN

The father is suffering horribly in his rumpled bed. At first his pain is still unconscious: in fact he continues to sleep and he is merely tossing and turning in his sleep – something from which he wishes to free himself, groaning. He wakes up only after a while and slowly becomes conscious of the fact that what is making him suffer is not a nightmare, it is a physical pain.

Then, with great difficulty, he decides to get up from his bed and to leave the bedroom very quietly so as not to waken Lucia.

From the room he goes along the corridor, which is still dark, almost groping his way and reaches the bathroom.

Here the shutter has been left open and through a gap in the curtain the early morning light, dazzling and already as unwavering as if it were midday, breaks in. Humble and supreme. But that sun, which is so marvellous – which *by chance* floods the house's white and shoddy space with the same innocence as it shines in the sky or among natural things – has for the first few moments no reality for the father; he is only uncomfortably blinded or feels in it only something that seems to increase his pain to the point of vertigo.

So covering his eyes with his hand he launches himself into an attempt to free himself of this suffering while above him – he no longer has even the strength to hold up his head – the sun continues to blaze through the little bathroom window from the brief, clear-cut radiant strip of garden which he glimpses through the gap in the curtain.

Only when he feels some slight relief does the father begin to become aware of the miracle of that brightness.

And his hand, still as if it were independent of his will, grips the window-sill uncertainly, searches for something on the windowpanes, draws aside the curtain, which is still shut on something consoling and astonishing – the light which he has never before seen at this time of day.

Thus almost all the garden behind the house appears – with the big green lawn and the clumps of laurels and birches he can glimpse round the edges – a silent corner of the world, over which that sun broods, sweet and deep, not seen and not enjoyed by anyone.

Then the father (he has never done such a thing in his whole life) comes away from the window, leaves the bathroom and once more enters the sad shadows of the house, walks through it, feeling his way, still in pain, until he opens the big glass door on to the garden and goes through it.

Walking on the damp grass, searching among the trees, he has on his face, which is struck by the sun (of a pink that is pure light), a slight, amazed and almost theatrical smile, so powerful is the enchantment. He walks along as if he were a stranger in some place he had never seen.

In fact for the first time he is noticing those trees touched by a light which lies outside the traditions of his experience. They seem, in fact, to be animated, like conscious beings – conscious and (at least in that peace, in that silence) fraternal. Passive under the light which touches them like a natural miracle, the laurel, the olive tree, the dwarf oak, and further off, the birch trees, seem to be content with a glance in order to repay that attention with an infinite and infinitely pre-existent love; and they say so, literally say so, by their simple presence, gilded and enlivened by the light, which expresses itself without words, but only through itself. *A presence which has no meaning and which is nevertheless a revelation.*

There is evidently no proportion between revealed miracles and all the other things we do in life. And yet the father – perhaps because for him they are already an extraordinary exception, these minutes passed wandering in his garden at that time of day – is unable to continue to live up to that situation, to struggle much longer with the sun's stupefying love; the cold makes him tremble painfully under the light material of his pyjamas, his feet are wet with dew, the pain in his stomach begins to make itself felt again.

So, still with his astonished and miserly smile on his lips he goes back into the house.

17

ENTIRELY MIRACULOUS LIKE MORNING LIGHT
NEVER SEEN BEFORE

Leaving the garden to its light, here is the father feeling his way once more in the opposite direction through the interior of the house until he turns down the corridor which is sadly lit by electric light. But, as if halted by an unexpected thought, he stops at the door of his son's room.

And again it is something mechanical and inspired that impels him; a kind of curiosity he has never felt before and which he is unable to wonder at – very quietly with a thief's caution he opens the door.

In the bedroom *that* light, having not yet completed to the full its task, which is unrelated to the things of this world, enters by the slits in the great shutters and outlines the guest and his son asleep in the same bed.

Sleep has disturbed their bodies, but it is a lack of composure that is full of peace. Their bodies, half uncovered, are entwined, but sleep separates them; their limbs are warm with an intense and blind vitality and yet they seem not to have life.

Touched, the father stands looking for a long time at this apparition to which he cannot give any meaning yet which is also in some way revealing.

He moves away at last, shuts the door very quietly like a thief and turns back to his room.

Lucia is sleeping her light sleep. His bed is disgustingly unmade. He goes and slips into it but he does not manage to get to sleep again. Something that has no name but only an unbearable lucidity causes him to lie there with open eyes thinking, perhaps, of a life whose meaning, having been deeply changed, now remains in suspense. What to do with it?

Suddenly seized by a kind of impatient madness he shakes Lucia and wakes her.

As far as she can grasp, he is asking her (having lost any sacred fear of the absurd and the ridiculous) to make love, at once; indeed he demands it.

Lucia does not realize what is happening – and he is already on top of her, violent, like a blind man groping as he runs; it no longer matters what she may think. But Lucia, who is terrified, is already immersed and lost in a questioning process which now concerns all her future life – something which at the moment when it happens is apparently without remedy: a new light that illuminates the past without a shadow of reason and pity.

Pressing himself against her belly, kissing her on the mouth and neck with ridiculous violence, without regard for her, as many times before, he blindly tries to prepare himself to make love. But in the end he has to give in to the prostration to which his terrible morning pain has reduced him all trembling: he remains lying on Lucia for a little longer like a dead body – then he separates himself from her, without looking at her and goes and lies down on his bed, humiliated and still in a state of excitement.

He remains there, overcome once more by the pangs of pain which he tries to hide, pale, exhausted by weakness, parched, looking at the void which is now full of the breath of the light, which is no longer that miraculous light of morning but the disgusting one of everyday.

18

THE GRACE AND CLOWNING OF THE
'DISPOSSESSED OF THE WORLD'

The morning is far advanced, the sun is already strong. The trees have lost their mystery, that sense of brotherhood of theirs – they are once again shut away in their simple silence (which is savage and inexpressive), oppressed by something greater than themselves and to which they humbly surrender.

In this sun, which is already high (high for the boss who is sleeping late – but in reality it is only nine o'clock in the morning), the postman Angiolo arrives – arrives without a hint of anything out of the ordinary about his gaiety which comes from other worlds, from other peoples.

Emilia appears to open the door to him – the postman gives her the first post – she takes it, then there is their usual little mute dialogue. Angiolino makes a few clownish grimaces with his mouth which serve above all to make him laugh. The rascal, this is the way he usually teases the peasant servant-girl . . .

But this time – a miracle! – Emilia opens her mouth, emits a human sound, utters words . . . As if it were an affair of state the curly-headed postman thus comes to learn that there exists a problem which is confided to him.

Delighted at the new perspective life is opening up for him, Angiolino then goes along behind Emilia with the kind of face suitable for great occasions. Emilia makes her way towards the interior of the house (so big that you could ride through the rooms on a bicycle, as Angiolino says). Until they arrive in front of the shoe-cupboard. The guest's shoes (which are, by the by, almost immaculate in their light colour) lie there questioningly before their eyes. They are of a kind Emilia does not know, modern shoes, as high as the calf and made of a material that certainly is not leather and not suede either: how to clean them? That is the problem. But Angiolino's eyes are laughing because he, who knows about modern things, knows that there is a special brush for these shoes but that in any case you can use any sort of brush. Diffidently Emilia tries and together the two of them, allied for once, busy themselves with the precious shoes.

When things seem to be well in hand and their problem happily solved, Angiolino leaves: forgetful of everything, he disappears towards those other places, those other peoples, those other worlds to which he is dispatched.

Emilia goes on cleaning the shoes lovingly and the moment her masterpiece is finished, very quietly, as if bearing a secret gift, she goes along the corridor (where the father had passed at dawn) and lays them in front of the door of the room of the young master and the guest.

19

BREAKFAST IN THE OPEN AIR

The whole family – as on the fine summer days when the holidays have not yet begun – are breakfasting in the open air. Emilia serves them.

They are all silent, the only sound – it sounds radiant – is that of a stupid distant radio.

Although they hide an unshared secret, the glances of Lucia, Pietro and Emilia, which they have only for the guest, are full of trepidation and purity. Only Odetta, shut away in her sulky pallor (that of a little white rabbit) seems to ignore him; and does so almost openly. But this terrifies her. So only she is lost in other thoughts and has no glances to give to the guest. Because the father too – still white and worn out after the vicissitudes of the night – has a way of looking at him which he certainly had never had before.

20

CAN A FATHER BE MORTAL?

The father is lying in bed, ill. Around him are his wife, his children and the guest. They are all gathered there for the visit of the doctor who in silence is going through his exact and consolatory gestures (it is a case of hypodermoclysis). The father's illness is not really serious but he is, as it were, far away somewhere, in a kind of mysterious walk-out; turned into a child by the illness and the pain, which at certain moments are intolerable, at others less so; in any case, an obscure and constant mood of obstinacy dominates him, almost in spite of himself, in his searching eyes: the desire to be saved.

The doctor leaves; Lucia and Pietro follow him in silence. So Odetta and the guest are left in the father's room. In fact Odetta never for a moment leaves her father's pillow; she has set up her tents there and does not intend to move away. She acts as his nurse, as faithful as a little nun in the odour of sanctity. And it has to be said she *truly* behaves in all respects in the best possible way. Meanwhile, her fear does not prevent her from acting in line with her inevitable sense of humour and then her habitual uncertainty when doing anything, now becomes tenderly brave in her successful effort to do everything equally well.

Yet her father's anxious glances are very seldom cast at her (they rest on her only every now and then with old tenderness); they are all aimed at the guest. It is the guest her father seeks the moment his wife and son have left the room with the doctor. Odetta knows this because from the first days of his illness her father has had an absolute and almost infantile need always to have the boy near him.

Now, in the way he looks at him, with the pleading glance of someone asking another for a sacrifice – because of a selfishness of which he himself is the victim – there is a kind of light, almost a slight smile.

The expression in his sick eyes is that of the moment when one suddenly understands something that brings relief to oneself (and above all) to anyone who is near: something that resolves a situation that is embarrassing and, in short, also slightly ridiculous.

He stretches out his big hand, which is weighed down by his illness, on the bed-cover, reaches a book, grasps it, raises it to his eyes and after looking for the page with some difficulty, begins to read with the uncertain voice of someone weakened by anaemia: . . . *But even in this unpleasant function Ivan Ilyich found a certain comfort. It was Gerasim, the peasant boy who waited at table, who always came to clear away. Gerasim was a clean, fresh, young peasant . . .* They are words from a book by Tolstoy, *The Short Stories*, open at a page of 'The Death of Ivan Ilyich'.

Laboriously, the father holds the book out to the guest for him to continue reading. Lightly, the guest takes it and at once plunges into it: '. . . *always happy, serene. To begin with the sight of this man, always cleanly dressed in the Russian manner, carrying out this repugnant task disturbed Ivan Ilyich.*

Once, getting up from the close-stool and incapable of pulling up his trousers, he let himself fall onto the soft couch and began to look with terror at his own naked thighs, the muscles standing out clearly, powerless.

Gerasim came in with his big boots, spreading around him the pleasing smell of fresh spring air, with a light and firm step and without looking at Ivan Ilyich – evidently restraining the joy of life that shone in his face, so as not to offend the invalid – and went towards the close-stool.

'Gerasim,' said Ivan Ilyich weakly, 'please help me, come here.' Gerasim approached him. 'It's difficult for me by myself and I have sent Dmitri away.'

Gerasim came close to him. With arms as strong as his step was light, he grasped him, lifted him up skilfully, with tenderness, and held him on his feet; with his other hand he slipped on his trousers and tried to make him sit down. But Ivan Ilyich asked him to take him to his divan. Gerasim, without effort, as if he were not even gripping him, guided him, almost carrying him, to the divan and made him sit down.

'Thank you . . . how skilfully and nicely you do everything.'

Gerasim smiled once more and wanted to leave the room. But Ivan Ilyich felt so good with him that he didn't want him to leave.

'There, bring that chair over to me, please. Put it under my legs. I feel better with my legs up. Can you hold up my legs yourself?

'Why not? Of course I can.' Gerasim lifted up his legs and began to talk to him. And – this was strange – he seemed to feel better while Gerasim held his legs.

From then on Ivan Ilyich took to calling on Gerasim every so often, rested his legs on his shoulders and liked to talk to him. Gerasim did all this without embarrassment, willingly, with simplicity and a goodness that moved Ivan Ilyich. Health, strength, vigour in all other men offended him; only the power, the vigour, the life in Gerasim did not make Ivan Ilyich feel bitter but calmed him . . .

21

THE CEREMONIAL OF A SICK MAN
(WHO HAS REGRESSED TO BEING A BOY)
AND OF A HEALTHY BOY
(PROMOTED TO BEING AN OLD YOUNG MAN)

The father is groaning on his tumbled bed; it is one of the
moments when his guts seem to come up into his throat and
an inhuman pain makes him gasp.

Dazed by that pain of his, he performs all the miserable
and humiliating acts which no reserve, no shame, and no
good breeding can now make him capable of repressing or
hiding.

Odetta's heroic eyes look at him impotently. Then the
bedroom door opens and the guest enters. Odetta's eyes turn
to him – but immediately turn back to her father's tortured
body.

The guest's body is like a carnal inspiration, full of physical
well-being and therefore also – because of the cruelty of just
things – moral. With that body of his, intact, the measure of
another world – that of a redeeming innocence – the guest
sits down on the edge of the bed, ready for his task, with pity
perhaps, but without any humiliating compassion.

The father has already caught sight of him, as if in a dream,
his eyes troubled and full of the poor abject sense of someone
who is in the hands of others; he has already made his
calculation and is waiting . . .

Then the youth – with what seem to be habitual actions –
helps him to take his legs one at a time from under the sheets.

He does it slowly between one pang of pain and another, born from the depths of the father's sick entrails, making him contort his lips, casting a veil over his eyes, squeezing the sweat from his white brow. Then very slowly, one at a time, with the painful collaboration of the sick man, he shoulders his legs, holding them at the ankles with his hands.

In front of him – a young peasant looking at him with the slight veil of irony in his eyes and that calm maternal care of his – the father, like Ivan Ilyich, is upturned on the bed with his head lost in the pillow; but relieved from the pain – or so at least he believes – he looks into the guest's face (it is unwrinkled and unflushed) between his legs which are painfully resting on his shoulders – he looks at his consoling health, his youth whose future seems endless. He smiles very slightly at himself, at his illness, at his alienation, at his need for help.

22

THROUGH THE EYES OF THE FATHER IN LOVE

So the summer sun was still there, triumphant, in the garden, which by now was facing the end of its glory, the first rust colours which are so poetic in the grey lights of the Lombardy air.

Between the shade, which is still warm, and the sun, which is so longer so scorching, the father is lying on a deck-chair, filled full of happiness, enjoying the world.

Near the convalescent father, reading, are the guest and Odetta.

But while the guest is really deep in his reading, Odetta is pretending to read, from time to time almost hating the book she has in her hand.

Her eyes roam uneasily over the things which for her father are charged with meaning – so much so that they almost explode with it in the intensity of the light – and which to her are merely boring and painful shadows. But more often still her glance is on her father's rested face.

Illness has transformed him and has certainly touched – before Odetta's eyes – a reality which seemed incorruptible: *the reality of the powerful and potent father.*

Suddenly Odetta's devotion for him is no longer mythical – as during her long, long infancy which does not wish to die – but, measured against reality, has now become uncertain and dramatic: it is the moment when love either grows or ends.

Perhaps this is why Odetta's glance escapes from the

extraneous words of the book and turns to questioning the face of this new father lying in front of her.

And there her father's eyes open, vivaciously and, as always, come to rest on the guest's face. Odetta once more follows his glance; but whereas up to now she had quickly moved it away from the guest to return to her father, instead it now remains there for the first time observing that young man whom she has always ignored. She is, after all, now seeing him for the first time.

What the father wants to ask the guest is what he is reading, a question lacking in curiosity, asked out of pure liking, from the fullness of the heart and the wish to speak. The boy raises those heavy blue eyes of his from the slim volume of Rimbaud he is reading and without any surprise, in his slightly hoarse voice, begins to read exactly those words at which, by chance, he had arrived.

Then, while he is reading – with one of those silent and graceful whims which are part of her life as a young girl – Odetta abruptly gets up, laying her book on the seat and disappears into the house. But not for long – in fact she comes out again with her camera, the one dedicated to the cult of the family and her father: the guardian cult (so often entrusted across the centuries to virgins).

Detached and obstinate she begins to take photographs – photographic souvenirs of the days of her father's convalescence. She puts her eye to the aperture and, click! she snaps her little picture, which will be a rare piece for the album.

But unlike what would have happened even a short time ago, Odetta does not choose as the only protagonist in the photograph her convalescent father. The unexpected discovery – although made through her father's eyes – of the guest's presence, is now a fact that cannot be eliminated, which not only imposes itself on her as something new but seems actually to render her incapable of mastering herself. Through the small square eye-piece she watches him unseen. She sees what his face is like, his shoulders, his broad chest and his slim pelvis, which is that of a young parent; his absentmindedness conceals a violence of which he seems, innocently, not to be conscious, or else of which only he knows the naturalness.

Odetta suddenly stops taking photographs and simply looks at the guest who, in his turn, raises his eyes to her.

But Odetta does not wish this, does not accept it. With the vehemence of her neurotic and impenetrable grace (like a little statue) she runs off; she goes and lays her camera down in the house.

Then she comes out once more and plants herself, expressionless, in front of the guest and takes him by the hand. She forces him in this way to follow her. He gets up obeying this modest invitation, this naïve ceremonial and, crossing the garden, follows her to her little bedroom.

23

A GIRL IN THE DEN OF VIRILITY

It is not really her little bedroom but the little room of when she was a little girl, now abandoned, with the dangling curtains, a white bed that is a little too pretty and a dark wooden trunk under the window.

The guest sits on the edge of the bed somewhat uncomfortably because the bed is high; so he has to remain like that, with his legs stretched out a little and parted. Thus when Odetta, after throwing a glance at him which is devoid of anything except the mad suspicion of a wild animal, leans over the chest, takes out of it her precious albums and turns towards him, she can do nothing other than sit between his legs with her back leaning against the bed. Or rather she nestles down there, for the boy's legs, encased in light taut cloth, are like two columns between which Odetta, that wild thing, can settle down naturally and with a kind of capricious elegance. It is true that were she to turn round slightly, she would find herself facing his loins, immaculate and powerful between the two protective columns; but she does not turn round. Her glances pass almost beseechingly from the photograph album to the guest's face and he is smiling at her, good-natured in his power.

She raises the great orbs of her eyes to him with her mouth half open – the mouth of a bewitched adenoidal child; then she lowers her eyes to the album once more and turns the leaves searching, with meticulous care that is the same as detachment, for the other show-pieces among her family souvenirs.

And the guest smiles at her. Then one of his hands with a gesture that is natural and unremarked, places itself on his thigh, on his lap, behind Odetta's head. At this gesture she turns her head and looks at the hand with that meticulous detachment of hers – then she looks up at him, careful not to change her expression and to maintain the same light in her eyes. But he smiles at her, fatherly and motherly, more warmly, and as if she were something dead and inert, catches her under the arms and pulls her up from the ground, raising her to his height.

The photograph album rolls to the floor and the two mouths meet. It is Odetta's first kiss and she receives it rigid and full of the intensity of her flesh, kneeling, held up by the powerful arms of the boy for whom she is so light.

24

'THE FIRST PARADISE, ODETTA'

The First Paradise, Odetta, was that of the Father.
There was an alliance of the senses in the child
(male or female)
due to the adoration of something unique.
And the world around
had only one feature: that of the desert.

In that obscure and endless light
in the circle of the desert, like a potent womb,
the child enjoyed Paradise.
Remember – there was only a Father (not the Mother).
His protection had a smile, adult but youthful
and slightly ironical, which is always that of the protector
of the weak, the fragile – male or little female.

You have been in this First Paradise
until today; and, being a female,
you will never lose the memory and veneration of it.
You will be by nature a worshipper . . . but before
turning to you to warn you of the dangers
of religion, I want to tell you the story
of your brother, who is of the same sex as God.
He too in the days when he was *really* a child
(more of a child than when he was in the maternal womb
or when he sucked the first milk from the breast)
lived in this First Paradise of the Father.

Hatred sprang up unexpectedly and without reason.
The loins which had been like a sun covered by
sweet and powerful clouds, the loins of that Man
immense and unique like the desert,
became a dark, deep spot in his trousers,
became wretched, lost its innocence
under the suspicion of being merely human.
The day had come
when the pure horizon of the desert is lost
in a silence and a less perfect colour
and the first palm-trees begin to be seen
and the first track appears silently among the dunes.

Thus the boy-child crossed the frontier of the First
    Paradise:
which remained behind in time; in the time (*dreamt of*)
of a green zone striped with transparent rows
of poplars – or in a great provincial city.
The child fell headlong to the ground,
lost the name of Lucifer and took, together,
that of Abel and that of Cain (so it is at least
in certain pink Mediterranean lands and in those green
    ones
where the nuns teach this to an Odetta ignorant of
    religion).

These lands were the Second Paradise.
There was a Mother (call her adoptive) who, in your case,
had rich furs redolent of precocious spring times.
How earthy, sweetly earthy,
was her sweetness – that of a petty bourgeois girl –
who does not desire all the precious things learned for
    herself

but for that little son of hers who walks at her side,
he too pearled with the freshness of primroses.

A river (in your case the Po) ran through this paradise:
because the house where your 'adoptive' parents live
after their marriage is always near a river.
Or if it is not a river then the sea or a chain of hills.

Fruits with stupendous names grew on their own:
apples, grapes, brambles, cherries and the flowers, the
    useless flowers,
were no fewer than they: and their names too
were marvellous, primroses, of course, or sunflowers
or snowdrops, or lily of the valley and even, for festivities,
    orchids.
The sun up there was certainly a friendly creature
made sweeter by the innocent idea the mother
communicated to her little son whose hand she held;
and how it was born in the morning, died in the evening,
making way for those stars which the son, obediently,
was barely allowed to see and must soon leave to their
    silences.

But that Mother was not, as he believed, innocent!
And so the same unreasoning hatred – which was born of
    itself
like a fruit or a flower in the First Paradise –
was also born in the Second. Our existence
is merely a mad process of identification with that of those
    living beings
whom something that is immensely ours sets us beside.

Thus we were the sinful Mother faced by the fruit

whose mystery reawakened the days of the First Father
so much further back than those of the green paradise of
  Lombardy.

The desert sun shone once more
on that little apple, the desire of modest existences.
The usual sun of every day stood to one side,
set apart as if in a sudden December; while the other,
burned tremendously – a measure against which to
measure centuries and miseries.
So the Mother *who was no other than her own son*
with maternal innocence and filial heedlessness bit into
that summer fruit. At once the Second Father, the
  adoptive one –
who compared to the first was like the weak
winter sun compared to that of the First Summers –
followed her example, erring man of the earth,
easily tempted, easily corrupted.

But with him too we had identified ourselves:
because, simply as ourselves, we could not exist;
we could exist only if we were Father and Mother.
We sinned with their own mouths, their own hands.
And the First Father chased us from the Second Paradise
  too.

So they are two – the Paradises we have lost.
With our parents holding our hands we take the roads of
  the world.
Lucifer distinguished himself from Abel and followed his
  destiny
finishing in the blackest darkness. Abel died,
killed by himself with the name of Cain.

In short there remained only a son, *an only son*.

After many thousands of years there was the first sowing
and another thousand years after that event
a King was named lord of all the men who had multiplied.
Oh how many coloured vessels! We had to earn our bread
and this began to take us from ourselves, to lose
each one in a false idea of Self, in the present Hell.
And that is the road your brother Pietro is taking.

But why, when explaining to you this Theory of the Two
    Paradises
have I spoken of your brother Pietro and not of you?
It is simple: because without his story of the male child
yours could not be compared with anything
and one could not therefore even to begin talking about it.

There was no female Lucifer, no female Abel and no
    female Cain;
so you should have remained in the First Paradise.
Or at least it is what you should remember, along with the
    true Father:
and so it is in fact – that is why you are immensely older
than your adoptive Father, with whom you are in love,
than your adoptive Mother, who is called Lucia,
and than your brother Pietro, the model for the whole of
    life.

With each of them you have identified yourself, poor
    thing;
and do not know that instead down there, before their
    birth,
you are the only one truly obedient to the First Father.

What must be more important – your identification or
   your being?
You are unable to choose, tender Odetta, because you are
   blind;
and thus you are chosen; thus you have lived; and you
   struggle
in vain against it, lost in a memory that is too beautiful
and a reality that takes you from dreaming to madness.

25

FROM POSSESSOR TO POSSESSED

The father and the young guest are in a car (the Mercedes of the father and factory-owner) which is running along the long, narrow tarred roads in the countryside south of Milan.

But at this point we think it is justified to stop calling the father simply 'father' and call him by his name which is Paolo. Even if a baptismal name, any name, can seem absurd if given to a father. It, in some way, deprives him of his authority, deconsecrates him, thrusts him back into this old state of being a child, exposing him precisely to all the wretched, obscure and anonymous vicissitudes of sons.

In fact, between Paolo and the guest there is an embarrassed silence although, to tell the truth, the only one embarrassed is Paolo; the guest, indeed, confines himself to remaining silent, delicate and obedient – he is truly a son and has every right to be so – one in whom the quality of father is potential and future and therefore all the more present and certain. So that behind the youthful, heedless and generous mask of the son there is a father both fecund and happy; while behind the marked, worried and avaricious authoritarian mask of the father there is an evasive and worried son.

At some point or other on the road – a deserted spot – the Mercedes stops, the father abandons the wheel and gets out, climbing in again by the other door and the guest, with pleasure (like all boys of his age), takes his place at the wheel. Inevitably, the moment it begins to move the car goes at least twice as fast. The transparent cathedrals of poplars against the ashen sky, which is still damnably cold, swallow it up more and more greedily, towards a south where there is no sun but, on the contrary, the irrigated meadows as they grow darker seem to have already taken on the colour of evening. It is the low-lying plain which instead of giving the North an opening towards a more joyful and sensual South seems to surround it like a moat. It is precisely towards this plain, towards the dense and wild thickets of the Po, towards the copses which can be so tenderly warm in the first still cold days of spring that by tradition lovers are instinctively drawn.

The conversation that Paolo wants to confront is undoubtedly serious (the youth is a little distracted by driving, by the ambition to take the corners well): but he does not have the courage for it, exactly like a boy.

To talk? Or should he too not rather *act before deciding*? Is he not with respect to his son and his wife the champion of a sense of authenticity which makes a man into a bourgeois man, carved in his respectablity and his rules (which by now are natural) like a marble statue? To speak of problems rather than of true feelings or of desires – is that not yet another excuse?

The guest's body is next to Paolo, intact and strong like that of a peasant; and moreover it has that prestige which it derives from being a middle-class educated boy (and there-fore with a strong sense of his own dignity). In fact a peasant's body can be touched and caressed because it is defenceless, it is like a dog with its master, it has (in his presence) no moral principles to defend – above all it is incapable of irony – in short it is, perhaps even against its will, obedient.

Yet the guest's body, rich in flesh but without softness, abundant but pure, in short all filial fecundity, is burning there at his side, at the wheel as if naked, from the grace of the chest and the outstretched arms to the violence of the thighs caught in the caress of the almost summery cloth.

The father – Paolo – looks at him and *before having decided to do so* caresses him.

He passes his hand – which has only ever caressed his wife and a series of beautiful and elegant mistresses in the proper way – very lightly over his hair, his back, his shoulder. The guest smiles happily without any surprise, with a childish and generous smile.

On the contrary he turns to Paolo, thus giving to the caress he has received a joyous naturalness; he shows his gratitude; and he rewards him with his youthful gaiety – almost humbly, precisely like someone born into a lower class, he gives him to understand that there is no violation of anyone in that gesture which, to a middle-class person, is mad. Yet not even for an instant does there gleam in that smile the sweetness of someone who is giving himself. On the contrary there is only the certainty of the person who gives.

That makes Paolo even more of a son. That indecisive caress (from which his hand has at once drawn back) is not the sign of possession but a prayer to the one who possesses. Now Paolo is one of those men who are used to being always the possessors. All his life (by birth and class) he has always possessed; the idea has never occurred to him even for an instant not to possess.

26

THE YELLOW REEDS BY THE RIVER PO

Now the Po appears almost unexpectedly in one of its great bends, as wide as a piazza and melancholy (the current is puckered and yellowish because a flood is beginning, it runs past giddily in a kind of devastating concentration towards Cremona, towards Mantua, towards the East).

Its appearance had been hinted at by a thickening in the lines of poplars which had become almost a forest; and the poplars, not only the square fields contained by them, were greener almost as if spring was further advanced and sadder there. And yet a little sun had overcome the clouds, had thinned out the stagnating mist, had linked the enormous amphitheatre of poplars which extended below the dyke as far as the eye could see, in an intensely clear sky.

The car has stopped on the dyke; Paulo and the guest get out and are standing motionless for a moment up there in the sun. Then Paolo, almost smiling, having now definitely regressed to being an inferior, with his rich man's tanned face creased by imposing wrinkles, stays by the car, uncertain and shy, as if not knowing what to do, where to go. But the guest, he too smiling (with that smile of his of someone who loses nothing, indeed gives everything, but in so doing does not in any way stain with a trace of pride or disdain his candid grace), runs slanting down the dyke which is still yellow, dry and wintry, and having reached the bottom of the dyke, like a boy going to play football, pushes his way through the bushes which in a large clearing came down to the running waters of the river.

The earth is soft and perfumed – but not damp. So too are the bushes which are almost all still dry except for a few with scattered little white flowers. On the ground, on the scented humus of winter and spring, there are still the leaves of the previous year, rotten and hardened.

In this kind of great terrace beyond the dyke by the riverside there are ravines which cannot be seen from up above. The guest disappears into one of these ravines to reappear lower down and further off among the rust-coloured bushes, of a rust colour however that is about to gleam with new tender colours (only the elders are already blood-red). Then he disappears again in another ravine which is deeper still and which certainly comes down to the water's edge.

Paolo keeps on after him, walking on that earth where he had certainly not set foot for forty years at least (when he was a boy) – he is bewildered by it like an invalid just out of hospital in the sun. The fact that he had always played games in comfortable surroundings is of no help to him – there is a kind of deep-rooted hostility between his body and this no man's land which is so very slightly and yet so very profoundly perfumed.

When beyond the second ravine, which he climbs down with difficulty, he reaches the guest, he finds him stretched out on the ground with one hand under his neck and in the other a lit cigarette (lit with a slight abandon and a little wickedly) and with his legs spread wide apart. Paolo goes up to him as if feeling a reverential fear for his abandon which is both arrogant and innocent . . .

27

'THE JEWS SET OUT . . .'

The Jews set out towards the desert.

All day long from when the horizon with its flat, dark, rocky dunes or those of sand, dark too, and rotund, stood out against the red of the dawn, to when it stood out once again in the same way against the red of the sunset, the desert was always the same.

Its inhospitality had only one form. It repeated itself in the same way wherever the Jews found themselves, whether halted or on the march.

At each mile the horizon was a mile further off – thus between the eye and the horizon the distance never changed. The desert knew only the changes of the desert – now it was a rocky plateau, now a stretch of boulders (enormous and naked as on the outskirts of the metropolises, with the same faded steely colour), now a lake of dark sand bordered by an infinity of rims that were capricious and all the same. But these variations took place in the midst of what was desert and only desert and resembled nothing other than desert. And these variations of rock, stones, or sand, were no more to the Jews than the sign of repetition, the possibility of perceiving a monotony that went into the bones like the fever of the plague. So the landscape of what was contrary to life repeated itself unshadowed and quite uninterrupted. It was born of itself, continued by itself and ended in itself; but it did not reject man, indeed it welcomed him, inhospitable but not hostile, opposed to his nature but not to his reality.

So walking across this vastness, it was as if one were always in the same place, coming again on the same dune, after a mile or a hundred miles, with the same wrinkles, all identical, drawn by the wind, not distinguishing any difference between the horizon to the north and that to the south, a little stone placed on the profile of a dune appearing to be equally vast whether in front or behind and all the ravines dug out of the arid colour of coal always the same ravines – the Jews began to form the Idea of Oneness.

They became aware of it the first day after walking fifty miles into the desert; they were engulfed by it on the second day after having covered another fifty miles without anything having changed. Until they had no other idea than that.

The Oneness of the desert was like a dream that allows no sleep and from which one cannot waken.

The desert was One and a step further on was One, two steps further were One – One for all the steps the Jews could take. The shapes of the palms, of the waters, the wells, the roads, of houses, were slowly lost from memory until the whole complicated business of the human world was left behind and seemed to exist no longer.

The Oneness of the desert was always there before the eyes of the Jews yet they contrived not to go mad. Indeed they felt themselves welcomed by that One thing that was the desert which they were crossing consciously but basically, by now, happy that they would never more be able to emerge from its infinitely distant frontiers. The habit of the idea of Oneness which the desert assumed in the senses, projecting itself like something that does not change in the inner being of whoever crosses it and without being able to emerge from it any longer (although it is entirely open) and however great the efforts he makes cannot forget it even for an instant – the

72

habit has become almost a second nature, coexisting with the first and little by little corroded it, destroyed it, took its place – just as thirst little by little kills the body that suffers from it. The Jews walked on and, even if they did not think about it, they were continually accompanied by the idea of so much darkness and so much light that had entered them.

So the Oneness in the design of the desert became something that was within those who suffered it. They were overwhelmed by it. It was the intolerable pain of a sick person who, racked with suffering, rolls from side to side in the bed and on the one side feels the desert and on the other still the desert and at the moment when he rolls over to change position feels at one and the same time the desire to forget it and to find it once more.

The Jews reached a new oasis along the course of a wadi. A few crows were flying about, there were camels grazing, nomads had pitched their tents round the well and stood there watching, interrupting their daily life for a moment with their eyes as sweet as those of precious dogs or gazelles.

But even in the circle of the new variety of life, that had been rediscovered – lost and ruminant in the profound peace of the sun – the idea of the desert remained within the Jews; it was nothing other than something Unique.

Moreover one had only to turn round and behind some palms, some low wall, or some rocky crest where the village of a tribe of a different race clustered, and it was there.

The apostle Paul who has the same name as the father set out from the oasis – from the city of sand, lonely as a cemetery, around its well and the life of which consists only in not dying. The mortal sickness was to be seen in the greenish waters of the well, in the decrepit old age of the trunks, in the dust inflamed by the sun in which everything had been crumbling for thousands of years. Yet there there was human life in all its forms and, although apparently stupefied or rendered mute by the silence that came from the desert, the small children laughed with eyes gleaming with sweetness and with their weightless bodies; the youths brooded over their lust among the rich rags and the tight bands tied round the sweet and repugnant lineaments of the bandits; the market hummed; groups of women returned from their purchases scurrying like so many old priests; the old men stood leaning in a row along the low walls with their rotten livers and their eyes like those of sick and tranquil animals.

The desert began to reappear once more in everything that existed – and in order to see it again like this – desert and nothing but desert – one only had to be there. Paolo walked and walked and each of his steps was a comfort. Once the last tufts of palms which had composed themselves into picturesque groups, had vanished, the obsession returned – that is to say a way of moving on while always staying in the same spot.

Yes, the desert with its horizon ahead and its horizon behind, continually unchanging, kept him in a state of delirium; every fibre in Paolo's body existed in its function – it was all dark stone or sand coagulated into furrows drawn by the wind, or grey dust with joints of metal where the wind raised regular and sinister streaks of a whitish cadaverous colour. Whatever Paolo thought was contaminated by that presence. Everything in his life (which was not – this now appeared clearly – the simple life of the oasis) was unified by that Thing which he experienced always in the same way because it is always the same.

He could not go mad because in the end the desert, in so far as it was an unique form, in that it was only itself, gave him a profound sense of peace – as if he had returned, no, *not to the loins of the mother but to the loins of the father.*

Indeed, as a father, the desert looked at him from every point in its horizon which was unconfinedly open. There was nothing that shielded Paolo from that gaze; at whichever point he was – that is to say always at the same spot – across the dark expanses of sand and stones, that gaze found him without difficulty – with the same profound peace, naturalness and violence with which the sun shone immutably.

The days and the nights passed.

And what was their purpose?

To cover and uncover a single Thing which was there in order to be covered and uncovered without anxiety across long twilights full of a melancholy that is completely without sound. That Thing did not, however, cause itself to be covered and discovered by night and day like an object but rather as a master who had himself decided on his own passivity, abandoning himself to that rhythm, the origins of which were equally deep in time as his own.

So when the sun was born again at an unmarked point on the horizon, suddenly, as if nothing real had happened, the desert was there all round with the lines and the light of the day before and with the terrible burning heat of the sun which came back to identify itself with danger and with death.

Paolo walked along that road without a history in that complete identification between the light of the sun and consciousness of being alive.

But how clean everything was, pure, uncontaminated! In that vital and ardent void the obscurities, the twists, the confusions, the contagions, the stink of life, were not even conceivable. Precisely because there was no variety only Oneness; the profound blue of the sky, the darkness of the

75

sand, the line of the horizon, the roughness of the terrain, were not forms that opposed each other, mutually exclusive, nor did they prevail over each other: no – they were a unique form and as such it was always present.

28

THE ANGEL'S SECOND ANNUNCIATION

Angiolino, as if playing *The Magic Flute* on an invisible and joyous flute arrives through the garden – presses his finger on the bell, waits, gives Emilia a glowing smile when she comes to open the door (since the guest has been in the house they have become friends), hands her first a rose, as a joke, then a telegram and leaves.

Our bourgeois family with its guest is at table just as it has been so often in the course of this story (the dinner is extremely tasteful, everything on the laid table could be a detail from a fresco of the times when production was human).

Bent over their plates each eats in silence. Each one cherishes internally their secret loving glances for the guest, like something that concerns him or her alone.

The common love for the guest in fact is not something that blinds them and before which all defences fall as on those occasions when we can naïvely find pleasure or suffer together.

All the members of the family have been made equal by their secret love, by the fact that they belong to the guest so that there is no difference between them. The glance of each one has the same meaning, the same end, but taken all together they certainly do not form a community of worshippers. (Even if the silence of that dinner of theirs is sacred.)

Emilia arrives in silence – she too with her secret which

makes her the equal of her masters, evidently, even while it leaves in her doglike poverty – and almost as it were her privilege hands the telegram to the guest. He reads the contents out loud: 'I have to leave tomorrow.'

APPENDIX TO PART ONE

THIRST FOR DEATH

I am destroyed or at least transformed
so that I do not know myself, because in me
the law is destroyed which –
up to this moment –
had made me a brother of the others:
a normal boy, or at least not abnormal,
or abnormal like everyone else . . . Even if
(need it be said) full
of all the errors that my class
and my social level within it
brings – which privilege compensates for.
In spite of this
before you entered my life –
putting it in doubt once more
and transforming it into a heap of rubble –
I was like all my companions.
So it is through the destruction of everything
that made me the same as the others
that I am becoming –
something unheard of and unacceptable – someone DIFFERENT.
This difference of mine, reveals itself to me unexpectedly:
up to this moment it had been hidden
by the unstable state of intoxication I had arrived at
(deceiving myself that I could be silent
about everything for ever), through your presence.
The one who made me different (a marvel!) has been near me.

And distracted me thus with the intensity and the unutterable
taste his sex had given my life.
The fear and the anxiety at not having you near me any more
to satisfy my desire, to see and touch you
when you are my comrade, but younger and fresher,
like a child, and more mature and powerful,
like a father who does not know how divine
his simple member is –
that is very difficult from the consciousness
of having to lose you for so long – perhaps for ever.
It is the consciousness of the loss
that gives me consciousness of my difference.
What will happen from this night on?
The pain of farewell goes beyond
this tragic sense of a future
to be spent in the company of a new Pietro,
completely different from me.
And what do your serious eyes, friendly and obscurely pitiless
(or already distant?), reply in silence to all this?
Is your intention perhaps
to push me along the road of difference,
to the end and without compromise?
Do you mean that if this love has been born
it is useless to turn back,
it is useless to feel it as a pure and simple destruction?
That, as far as the pain of separation goes,
I could find someone who could replace you,
and recreate in me those feelings
of ridiculous tenderness and animal passivity
so recently born and so brusquely interrupted?

*

And if you were a father without wrinkles and without grey hair,
a father as he was when he was little more than my age,
could there not be a father like that
to replace you? Even if
that is inconceivable and terrifying,
indeed, precisely for that reason?

IDENTIFICATION OF INCEST WITH REALITY

Is it not the things which seem most just and simple
that reveal themselves, in the end, to be the most obscure and difficult?
Is it not life itself, in its naturalness,
that is mysterious – and not its complications?
The farewell between you, who go away, and me, a young girl
whom you could marry only in a year or two
is the most tragic thing in the world.
And then . . .
Until your arrival I had lived
among – forgive the eternal word – normal persons
but I was not; and I had to protect myself
(and be protected) to hide
the painful symptoms of my class-sickness,
that is of the void in which I lived (a sinister health).
That sickness within me continually
threatened to come to light,
to unmask me and everything.
So things were to be taken . . . with a sense of humour –
like a boast, like an aristocratic habit
to be cultivated, little hot-house flower, in the warmth of the house.
Exactly (just imagine!) as if it were a case
of a ridiculous and rash openness
to anarchistic ideas, or slightly subversive ones, frozen places

certainly not visited by any of my peers . . .
You brought me back to normality.
You made me find the right solution
(a blessed one) for my soul and my sex.
The miraculous presence of your body
(which encloses an over-large spirit)
dispelled my wild and dangerous
little girl's fear . . . But now,
in this farewell, not only
do I fall headlong backwards
but I go further back still.
The pain is the cause of a relapse
More serious than the sickness
that preceded the brief cure.
The caresses you give me in silence,
perhaps to console me, perhaps –
with the cruelty of every logical act
to thrust me farther down and deeper
into my pain – have a meaning
that is absolutely obscure.
What are you trying to suggest to me and propose to me so
    mysteriously?
Perhaps someone who could take your place?
And this person could be someone
who, like you, replaces my father,
the father of Pietro, of the First Father?
And why not simply my father himself?
Are you trying to suggest to me by means of
terrible and mute words of justice
the identification of a truth,
always unimaginable and incestuous,
with the whole, the entire reality?

THE LOSS OF EXISTENCE

My husband's interest in his industry
was born with him, was indistinguishable from him.
It made one whole, together with something inexpressible
which was his life with his work.
Had he been born a peasant
he would have had the same interest in the earth
and the tools that serve to work it;
had he been born a sailor (up to a century ago)
he would have had the same interest in the sea and the ship.
In short, he has worked all his life
in a great industry inherited from this father
(its creator) driven on by a (natural) interest.
As in every historical period, ours too
has constructed nature and hence naturalness.
As a member of the upper class of Northern Italy
my husband lived his nature with naturalness
(almost as if, precisely, his factory
was like the land or the sea).
His interest in his own work
and in his own earnings (enormous
and, as our enemies define them, unjust)
is the same as drives us to act in our dreams.
Necessary and vague. In short, he
has never had an objective interest,
pure and cultural, in existence.
As for Odetta, are her family cults
objective, pure and cultural interests?
Yes, perhaps they have the naïvety,
the intensity, the lack of any advantage;
but ultimately they are like exorcisms
compared to a true religion,

or games compared to a real job.
She has constructed herself in the mould of such interests,
and with this mould she amuses herself
(perhaps feeling the void in them
and becoming aware of it only through suffering).
As for Pietro, he studies and is constrained to have
some obligatory interest in something,
even if only within the walls of our best city liceo.
These days
he is reading The Symposium . . . Can he do so
with complete impunity?
In short, in my family, we all live
in existence as it has to be:
the ideas by which we judge ourselves
and others, the values and the events,
are, as they say, a patrimony common
to all our social world.
I, in this sense, was the worst of all.
It is difficult to say how I lived;
how in order to live I required only the naturalness of living –
to think about my house, about my affections,
almost like a peasant woman in her family nest
who fights tooth and nail for existence!
How was I able to live in such a void? Yet I did live in it.
And that void, unbeknown to me, was
full of conventions, that is
of a profound moral ugliness.
My natural grace (it seems) saved me:
but it was a grace that was being lost.
Like in a garden, a spot where no one passes.
It was there . . . in my barbarian eyes (it seems)
in my mouth, in my high and sweet cheekbones . . .
in shapes full of a thinness (alas) of a

86

Mannerist adolescent . . . and probably, yes, was also
in my heart, which was timid, but capable of feelings.
Yet there it withered.
It was like growing old
(like the first excessive pallors, the first
accursed, still invisible wrinkles). It would have withered
till it was dry – coinciding with the end
of a useless life – had you not arrived.
You filled with a pure interest –
a mad one – a life devoid of any interest.
And you untangled from their obscure knot
all the mistaken ideas on which a bourgeois lady lives:
the horrible conventions, the horrible sense of humour,
the horrible principles, the horrible duties,
the horrible graces, the horrible affability, the horrible
anti-communism, the horrible fascism,
the horrible objectivity, the horrible smile.
Ah, what a lot I know about myself, you will say. It is a
    consciousness
acquired by magic – and I am speaking like the monologue
of a character in a tragedy!
Odd, my pain has the accents
of naturalness and truth,
which people normally have at the mortal moments of life;
it does not seem to challenge it. Perhaps because what
was destroyed in me by your love
was no other than my reputation as a chaste bourgeois woman.
Yet while you are caressing me, understanding and pitiless,
I wonder: What do you want to push me into?
Into something which if, on the one hand, it can in some way
redeem and console me, on the other hand, can it do other than
push me back more and more towards the precipice
which I had begun to reach

by deciding on my adultery with you?
Are you trying to tell me, boy that you are, that it is possible
to substitute for your body and your soul
the body and soul of a boy who resembles you?
That his eyes can have for me the blueish
light of desire mixed with tenderness?
And his coarse hands the rough and reverent
weight of someone who, as he caresses, hurts without noticing?
That he can be, in short, a man who has grown up before my eyes
like a son . . . until he became
the young barbarian who wants no obstacles to his mounting?
And why, if he has to be like my son in age
(his nakedness sacrilege, his erection impossible),
why not simply my son?
This absolutely extreme choice –
and one without any possibility of turning back –
is it the only act that can save a life
from the lack of any interest
and from the void filled with values which are all mistaken?
A moral shame pushed to the point
of touching and giving oneself to the most boyish boy of all –
one's own son becomes a man –
is it the only way to overturn all false justices
and to live, even if unjustly, in truth?
Are these things I can
even so much as imagine?

THE DESTRUCTION OF THE IDEA OF ONESELF

So you came into this house to destroy?
What did you destroy in me?
You simply destroyed –

along with all my past life –
the idea I have always had of myself.
So if for a long time
I had assumed the form I had to assume
and my figure was in some way perfect,
what now remains for me?
I can see nothing that can reintegrate me
in my identity. I look at you: you do not listen to me
impartially – because you do not divide yourself –
but with dedication, because you give all of yourself to everyone.
But how can your consoling presence
be so pure, so much as to display
almost a clear desire for detachment?
What is the use of consoling me if you, if you wished,
could postpone – perhaps for ever –
your departure? Instead you will leave;
of that there is not the least doubt.
So your pity is subordinated
to some other mysterious plan.
Are you, perhaps, trying to tell me (not by talking, but simply
by the fact of being a boy),
that you could be replaced now
by my son or my daughter?
A completely mad proposal (preordained)
perhaps by some obscure desire of mine)
and yet accurate if, although realized
(my son's naked member, my daughter's naked vulva),
it were only a symbol; and if, through it,
you were to exhort me to the most total perdition,
to place life outside itself,
outside order and outside tomorrow,
making of all this the only normality.
Perhaps because whoever has loved you must

(like every man – who does not know it),
be able to recognize life at any cost,
at every moment? Recognize it and not only
know it or merely live it?
Are they – you say generously in my banal bourgeois language –
the most unthinkable exceptional cases,
the most intolerable ones, the most remote from the possibility
of being conceived and actually named,
those that present themselves as the most effective means of
recognizing life?
Exceptional cases which however, can
only be symbols –
if in reality, like everything that is real,
they are made of nothing and destined to nothingness?

COMPLICITY OF THE SUB-PROLETARIAT AND GOD

I salute you last of all, just
five minutes before leaving,
because the suitcases are ready by now
and the taxi has been sent for?
The last and in haste: why? Perhaps because
your poverty and your social inferiority
have some value for me?
And so, in your case I spend less of myself
as if your body were of second quality
and your spirit had the restless way of jumping up,
stupid, angelic and sluggish, like an animal?
No, none of this.
I salute you badly in haste and last of all
because I know your pain is inconsolable
and you do not even have to ask for consolation.

You live entirely in the present.
Like the birds of the air and the lilies of the field
you give no thought for the morrow. But
did we ever speak? We did not
exchange words, almost as if the others
had a consciousness and you not.
Instead evidently you too,
poor Emilia, girl of little worth,
shut out, dispossessed by the world,
do have a consciousness,
a consciousness without words.
And consequently without chatter.
You don't have a beautiful soul. For all these reasons
the rapidity and the lack of solemnity
in our farewells are merely the sign
of a mysterious complicity between the two of us.
The taxi has arrived . . .
You will be the only one to know, when I have gone,
that I shall never return, and you will seek me
where you have to seek me; you will not even look at
the road down which I shall go, and disappear
and which all the others, on the other hand, astonished, will see
as if for the first time, full of a new feeling,
come into consciousness
in all its wealth and its ugliness.

PART TWO

1

EMILIA'S COROLLARY

Emilia, with a big cardboard suitcase in her hand, comes out of the house, shutting the door behind her in religious silence as if she were running away. In fact she is leaving in secret. She looks around her. There is a profound silence. She is still uncertain. She opens the door very slightly, looks in. The succession of corridors, rooms, right down to the big living-room flooded with sad sunlight, is entirely empty and deserted. She shuts the door again. A satisfied, hard expression like that of someone possessed distorts her face; there is also in that expression of hers a hint of holy cunning.

She goes down the stairs on tiptoe carrying the suitcase the way that peasants carry the pitcher from the fountain – all bent to one side with her arm pulled down, her hand red and swollen, shamelessly.

She walks the whole length of the path through the garden looking around her slily, gesticulating still more with her free left arm to keep her unsteady balance: but what is in that big cardboard suitcase? Lead? In it are her treasures and her memories, poor Emilia. She lugs them along heroically and by this time uselessly.

Now she is on the road. The same down which the day before, or some days before or, in short, some indefinite time before, the guest's taxi had disappeared.

There is the same silence, the same light. The inhabitants of that place are spending the day following the rhythms of similar ideals. Balconies and Liberty-style pergolas, twentieth-century hillocks, sharp corners of cement, tiled bays, rise towards the skies, above the little gardens with the dark stunted green of the little presumptuous pines and even of some horrible palms.

She makes her way down the long, straight line of the perspective, slowly, lugging her suitcase with her – it changes hands every so often – until she becomes tiny in the distance and disappears.

*

She reaches a big round piazza with, in the centre, a green lawn and around it streets like rays which all open out in the same way with the same perspectives. Big houses and under the boughs of the urban chestnut trees everything is blurred by the mist. Trams and buses circle the piazza without cease and rivers of cars; the noise of the engines is a never-ending din and now sirens also join in – the sirens of midday or of evening or of some other time at the factories. The people around Emilia seem not to hear or see anything; nor does Emilia. Under an arched shelter they all wait, diligent, absent and dignified, for the arrival of their means of public transport. Now it arrives, unwelcoming, obligatory, gleaming; now it sets off again with its new load, disappearing down of those streets which go off like rays from the great and crowded piazza towards a distance of floating clouds of haze.

*

Emilia is standing under another arched shelter – a bigger one this time, with a long wall behind it and stone seats. She has her feet on the battered suitcase. She clutches it tightly against her calf like a dog which does not for a moment lose sight of what has been entrusted to it. The people around her, who are also waiting with their suitcases, are more like her than the others. They are peasants like her who come and go from Milan from their little villages in the plain. The vehicle that now arrives is a big old bus which has almost outlived its time. It arrives after an interminable wait and after another interminable wait, when it has long been full of all these people who are withdrawn into themselves, almost as if in religious silence, it sets off again.

*

The bus stops in the little square on the edge of a village. The little square is all white, desolate. In one corner there is a pizzeria, opposite it a shop-window full of coffins, between them a bar with neon writing, gleaming windows and inside the old, stale, cold poverty of peasant life. From the door at the front of the bus a line of people slowly comes down – old peasants with jowls like pigs, women dressed in black, some students, a soldier, and at last, with her suitcase which makes her walk lop-sidedly, Emilia.

Her fellow passengers scatter in the silence of the village down long, narrow, ugly streets; ones that are carefully tarred and with the plaster on the houses from a century ago recently painted in bright, cold colours.

Emilia too disappears down one of these streets where there are only some children wrapped up in clothes that are not poor (like in fairytales) and a few dogs. At the far end one can see the countryside, a tremulous and transparent setting of poplars whose first green has the uncertainty of the colour of the earth and whose buds are still curled up and sparse like dry leaves.

A stupendous veil of mist makes of these rows of poplars, which appear far away, a setting that is excessively refined for a solitude sacred because it is the solitude of peasant life.

*

The landscape is the same as that through which some time before Paolo, the father, and the guest had ventured with their car as far as the Po, or, if you like the landscape through which Renzo reached the Adda on foot according to the story in Manzoni's most poetical pages.[1]

But there is something unnatural in the huge number of poplars which frame the fields and the sky, ahead, behind, to the right and left; patterns of poplars as big as parade-grounds or oriental squares or as narrow and measured as the ground-plans of cathedrals; and which shine through, one beyond the other, to infinity: a diagonal file shines through on to a straight file, a straight file on to a file parallel to it, and the latter on to a perpendicular file, and since the land is undulating, the way in which one row of poplars shines through to another has no end; it is an immense amphitheatre like those in old prints of battles and in the unnatural and profound peace (an unnaturalness and a profundity due certainly over and above to the work of nature – which is busy there, passive and potent, as at the bottom of a sea – but also to the wood-pulp industry) there appear here and there, like little heaps of precious objects, the severe belfries with, alongside them, the clumsiness of their dome of a reddish chestnut, almost rust-coloured, and with blood-coloured cracks (the bleak spots of the seventeenth and eighteenth centuries, now stagnating and awaiting their end).

It is across this countryside – down a long, narrow and

[1] A reference to the hero of Manzoni's historical novel *I Promessi Sposi* (*The Betrothed*) (Tr.).

carefully tarred road – that Emilia is now walking, lugging her suitcase behind her. She walks for a long time, stopping every so often and shifting the weight from one patient hand to another; alone in that vast expense of poplars, irrigated meadows, sky and hoardings. Until, having reached a little crossroads, where from the tarred road a dirt track of dark earth branches off with, in the centre, a long ridge of grass (the old cart-track), she changes direction and, hastening her step, makes for a farmstead which rises like a barracks at the end of the rows of poplars, against the melancholy green.

*

In the courtyard of the farmstead there is no one. A veiled sun fills it everywhere, almost without leaving a line of shadow in any corner.

Around it there are long buildings, low, with red roofs; on one side a long-roofed building with the byres (silent) standing in the shade of the round towers of two leaning silos, as severe as the belfries, which appear far off beyond the infinite rows of the poplars; on the other side, a house with the shutters all closed, where only the grey door with its glass panes is half-open but covered with a sad, immaculate curtain. In front there is a single house, perhaps another byre and a heap of red bricks among pieces of equipment, blood-red, which seem to be abandoned there for ever to rust; and between one building and the other (fantastical and fussy like princely barracks of the eighteenth century) there are the airy perspectives of the poplars in the mist, on undulations complicated by high banks, by towpaths, perhaps because of the presence of a river.

On a heap of sand in the middle of the courtyard, where there are still traces of a crumbling cement floor, two children are playing muffled up in clothes poor but clean, as in illustrations to fairy-tales. They have red and inexpressive faces – already adult and canny – like their peasant parents. With a curiosity that is unsurprised, perhaps because of shyness or good manners learnt at home or in the nearby elementary school, they watch Emilia arrive and enter that great courtyard in silence.

She in her turn looks at them in silence.

She had walked all that way lugging her suitcase behind her as if driven by the obsessive determination of a blackmailer, of an infanticide. Now she is there, unmoving, in front of the courtyard of her old home which her silence and her fear render still more sacred. A dog comes and sniffs at her.

She moves forward a few more steps towards the interior of the courtyard (while at the door one can already see the white embroidered curtain being raised and some worried and hostile faces squash themselves against the glass), forgetting for the first time to take up the suitcase which remains abandoned on the earth, swollen, alone and useless.

At the other side beyond the heap of red bricks and the bits of harness there is an old bench – burnt by the sun, rotted by the rain – which has been there perhaps since Emilia's childhood days. Recognizing it, it is this bench which she makes for, walking once more with her former obsessive, obstinate gait, and she sits down, remaining rigid and motionless, in the alien light of the sun.

2

ODETTA'S COROLLARY

The house is silent and deserted. True, it is always like this because it is very big for the few people who live in it, and Lucia had taken care to teach the servants to be silent and keep to themselves. Yet, now, in the silence and emptiness there is something special. As if the house were really uninhabited.

The guest seems not only to have taken away with him the lives of those who live there but he seems to have to divide them from each other, leaving each one *alone* with the pain of loss and a no less painful sense of waiting.

So Odetta gives the impression of being alone in the whole house. She goes backwards and forwards through it as if searching for something in the emptiness. But both the interior of the house and the garden appear to have fallen asleep in a definitive and indifferent silence.

Odetta's face during these vain expectations of hers remains impossible to read. On the contrary, a kind of good humour (a sly smile with a touch of humour at the back of her eyes) deforms her features ambiguously.

She goes to the end of the garden, reaches the point where she and her family, leaning over the low gate which is covered by creepers, had seen the guest for the last time, going away, disappearing; and she looks down the perspective of the empty street.

What she is searching for in this void is not clear. And that void is more sad, offensive, normal, than ever. Cement, expensive materials, gloomy spikes in Liberty-style, absurd and stunted conifers, are lined up down that long perspective without a single ray of hope or of reality.

Odetta observes it sardonically.

Then she turns on tiptoe and with an artificial and comical gait (a long stride like Puss-in-Boots) she regains the house. She almost runs across the last part. But having reached the centre of the drawing room she stops suddenly. She looks around her, pursing her lips (still in a very comical way) and almost emitting, with her lips shut and drawn tight, a kind of song. She stays like this for a long time. Then she moves again.

This time she goes into her father's bedroom. Where, however, she stays only for a moment. A moment, the time to count – fairly slowly however – to three: one, the place where her father lay, two, the place where she, Odetta, sat and three, the place where the young guest came and placed himself. Having given that lightning glance Odetta runs, literally runs out, into the garden, to the part where her father used to rest in the long wicker seat during his convalescence.

Here Odetta's examination of the scene is long and complicated. She looks at the spot where her father lay, the spot where the guest sat and the place where she sat.

There is no trace in the grass (it has grown almost wild again as in the beginning of time) of those 'far off' siestas, of those middays so profoundly enjoyed, where a life was reborn and a love born. But in Odetta, evidently, the memories are alive and clear.

She goes to the spot where her father lay and, trying to be as accurate as possible, paces out the distance from the spot where the guest sat; and then from the point where she sat. Then, still in the same way, she measures the distance between the spot where she sat and the point where the guest sat. But she is not content (she makes comical expressions of scepticism with her mouth, wrinkling her nose as well). Thus she disappears, running into the house and makes her way as far as the kitchen.

Then there is the new maid who, by a fluke that is undoubtedly not common, is called Emilia like the previous one. She is a girl who is no longer young; small (with a pale worn face and big pitiful eyes). Odetta asks her for a measuring-tape and the new maid, silent and quick, gives it to her.

With the tape in her hand, Odetta triumphantly returns to the garden. And there she starts her measuring again, this time with the accuracy of millimetres, breaking off to make rapid calculations, lost in thought and not without a hint of humour. She does not even fail to smile to herself.

3

AT THE FARMSTEAD

A pink moon is rising behind the rows of poplars – it doesn't even look like a moon but like a bleeding and shapeless piece of some big, soft, decayed body.

It throws on to the courtyard of the farmstead, where a little pearly lamp is also shining, a light of unbearable sweetness.

The farmbuildings stand around, reddish and corroded; in the semi-darkness their rustic quality has disappeared and the outline of those two silos, of those byres, of those walls of red bricks, is almost solemn.

In the midst of this sort of corroded stage-set, in silence, Emilia, is sitting on her bench – *in the same position she took up when she sat down.*

Her suitcase is no longer at the centre of the courtyard. A little light filters through the glass-paned door of the farmhouse and the clean white curtains are drawn up. Through the glass there are glimpses of the people of the house looking out – at Emilia of course. They are an old man, an old woman with a black headscarf, a young married woman, a man, still young but fat and too red, and at the edge of the glass down below the faces – they too are round and red – of the two little children, diligent and inexpressive. They are shadows – grey or barely tinged with pink – beneath the white of the curtains. The moon does not reach them; instead it makes the courtyard gleam with its crumbling cement, its piles of sand, its red bricks, like a little lake or like the precious ruins of an old church.

4

IN WHICH IT IS DESCRIBED HOW ODETTA
ENDS UP BY LOSING OR BETRAYING GOD

Odetta is now bending over a big trunk (in her little bedroom, the place where for the first time she discovered love, in the body of the young guest). This trunk Odetta is emptying completely with her new – slightly comical – detached patience with which she enacts these days of her life.

It is no easy business because in that trunk is contained all her childhood, represented by an infinite number of treasures, some easily recognizable, others only recognizable by Odetta and otherwise without meaning, value or even shape.

The trunk is emptying slowly until at the bottom, at the very bottom, and therefore literally buried, the photograph album appears. She takes it out, almost unceremoniously, in the way we fulfil habitual actions which no longer have charm for us, and begins to leaf through it.

She quickly comes to the pages where the photographs taken of her father and the guest are inserted – photographs, faded and out of focus, as if they were much older than they really are. Odetta takes a long look at them one by one (there are about ten of them).

In one, the guest has stopped reading the book he had been intent on, has raised his head and is smiling; in that position with an unintentional gesture that is youthful and virile, he has parted his legs; and the beauty of his body appears in all its aggression. Odetta runs her small thin finger over that body as if to recognize it and stroke it at the same time. It is a careful action but an uncertain and childish one which clumsily follows the outline of the figure photographed until it runs over the loins. But at this point Odetta suddenly closes her hand, clenching her fist.

She gets up, goes and throws herself on the bed with her face in the pillow. It is not clear whether she is weeping or doing it for a joke. But when, a long time later, she turns round facing upwards, stiffening herself on the bed, her expression is entirely changed; there are no longer any grimaces, smiles, simpers, flashes of humour – in short, distractions or defensive manoeuvres. She has become expressionless, motionless, thoughtful: she is looking up into space and only a kind of astonishment has not yet abandoned her to complete atony.

*

The darkness which is invading the bedrooms seems to have an almost conscious meaning: the passage of time, which follows a useless destiny of its own; the evening is made for urgent duties and anyone who falls short feels the pain of a freedom that seems atrocious. The dark is a lesson – a lesson that justifies the fathers and the fathers' fathers who preach normality and duty. In fact a bell is not lacking, even if a very distant one, and voices closer by (mixed perhaps with some indefinable music, the accent of family life at the end of a day of work) and also signs of life within the house.

But Odetta seems to be insensible to everything – to the tragic lesson of the dark, to the consolations it suggests, to the unfulfilled duties and to the terrible freedom of the void with which she has replaced daily life.

She stays still, stretched out on the bed, with her face turned upwards and her neck stretched out.

It is thus that the new Emilia finds her when she comes to call her to supper and turns on the light. A light that is truly inopportune and absurd because it reveals a reality which is not only more bearable but more true if protected by the dark.

So the new Emilia, who is worried – with her big eyes which in themselves are already perpetually terrified – shakes Odetta lightly at first and then, as far as respect allows her, a little harder. Touching her on the arms to persuade her to come to supper she notices – poor, new Emilia – that one fist, the fist of the right hand, is tightly clenched.

*

However illogical that may seem now, the whole family is round Odetta's pillow (it is day, the light enters triumphantly through the glass door). And yet each of them is alone, carrying out their family duties. There is also – indeed he is the protagonist – the family doctor who, as soon as his examination is over, looks at the poor little person lying there and, sceptical and sad, gathers up his instruments.

At the end of the arm outstretched at her side and held very close to the body – Odetta's fist.

Now in Odetta's life nothing changes any more: it has become stabilized and fixed forever in that absurd and deceptive manner. She is there, in her bed, motionless, her face looking up, her eyes without any sign of feeling, with only a little fear – staring into empty space and with her fist tightly clenched against her side.

Then the new Emilia enters the room (now empty) in terror, opening the door with the tact of poor peasants –

because she is a peasant – who always feel they are to blame and are always afraid of disturbing people. She comes in with her frightened eyes because, if this time she really were to blame, it would indeed be a great and terrible guilt.

She looks towards the bed where her young mistress is lying, then she looks out into the corridor, then at the bed once more where the unheeding body has not even noticed her.

From her mouth there comes a naïve and breathless call 'Signorina!' as if to warn her of a new danger or of a new pain. But her voice remains strangled in her throat and her eyes grow bigger, gleaming with frightened love.

At length she stands aside and two men (in that house they seem to belong to another species with the hard, massive features of a different race) come in, dressed in white, with a stretcher.

Using a tact which is only indifferent skill, they take Odetta's small body (as if it were an object) and place it on the white stretcher. So, as rapidly as they entered, they leave.

Outside at the far end of the garden another of them is waiting at the wheel of an ambulance which he starts up at once. The stretcher with its contents is placed in the vehicle and it goes off white and silent.

Quickly, in order to disappear, it enters the same street down which the young guest had disappeared one day: the street, which is always the same, in one of its silent and sad hours when nothing happens.

*

Now they are taking Odetta on a trolley down the white corridor of a clinic – a modern clinic, rich and welcoming. Along the corridor there are rapid glimpses of interiors

108

flooded by the midday light and by peace. A white bed with a white face. A white chair with a man in pyjamas sitting there. The gesture of a nurse restraining an invalid who wants to sit up, gesticulating and searching for something. A face listening, long and sly, as it lies on the pillow, watching the trolley pass by out of the corner of an eye.

At the end of the corridor is Odetta's room: the room where Odetta, who knows why, has wanted to finish up.

Tidy, gleaming, light, like all products of a bad conscience. Because there is no doubt that Odetta's 'dropping out'[1] find all Milan in agreement with it: there is a tacit understanding between her and the power (whatever that may be) that sets up clinics – a very expensive clinic in Odetta's case, given that there are differences between different ones.

What compelled Odetta to be so renunciatory? To enter into a treaty of alliance with her persecutors? To help by cutting herself off of her own accord, with such gentleness, such a desire to please, and, one might say, with such sly animal tameness, those who wish to exclude her? Why has she agreed to hush up the scandal which she herself caused with the same melancholy diligence with which she has always lived?

But there is really no reason to expect that now or in the future Odetta will wish to give any satisfaction to such questions: she shows that she simply is unconscious of the very people who from the trolley lay her on a bed.

What she diligently takes steps to do – naturally without noticing it – is to keep her fist tightly clenched and very close to her side.

Beside her bed there is a big window through which a light enters that is tender although bad.

---

[1] In English in the original (Tr.).

Through a window like that, one can enjoy a view extra-ordinarily like the one you enjoy from the garden of Odetta's house.

Of this road, from the big window, one sees only the right-hand side against empty space, because evidently the road falls away slightly and so everything ends with the sky (an everyday sky, perhaps grey perhaps blue, undoubtedly colourless). From that empty space a profound sadness is reflected onto the road – almost as if something were lacking in that void which ought instead to be happy; for example a promenade with a sweet and gentle southern sea for long, truly happy holidays. But that is not what counts; neither the reality of these houses – luxury buildings around a luxury clinic, nor the jealously granted privacy of those families of Milanese professional people or industrialists who actually keep the shutters closed and only the odd servant, who every so often appears for a moment to disappear once more into the impenetrable shade of the interiors.

None of this is important for, however, engimatic, it has a meaning, and, however sad, a history.

What is important is what is, and what is, is what seems to be. The apparition is mysteriously geometrical, even if it is irregular. Each point has an exact distance from every other point. One has to measure that distance – and it is a long task because the points are infinite; exactly one hundred and fifty, for example, are the windows (with the shutters shut or half-shut) of which forty have balconies. In one window a red carpet is displayed, dangling like a dead body. The tips of the trees – almost all conifers – which rise up from the little gardens underneath on the lower floors – are seventy-five in number. The corners of the house, thirty; the walls, twenty: three of these twenty walls are of small tiles of a tender hazelnut colour; seven are greyish or marble or artificial marble; six, rose-coloured, distant, and therefore difficult to decipher; four, of a colour between purple and pink, a livid colour, against which the dark Christmasy greens of the pines stand out.

The lamp-posts – arched at the top in an almost flirtatious manner as in show-grounds – with their opaque tube for the neon lighting are six in number; and they disappear down the hill towards the clinic. Perhaps at the end of this road there is a church because you unexpectedly hear the jangling bells calling people to service, in a lugubrious way, with the false exaltation of carillons.

Odetta's eyes look at this void filled by the apparition of that architecture and of these sounds. The fist at her side is tightly clenched.

5

PUSTULES

More time has passed. (Perhaps days have passed, perhaps months or perhaps even years.)

Emilia is still seated on her bench against the reddish wall full, up to her eyes and the roots of her hair, of madness.

Meanwhile, something has changed in the farmhouse, which is red, warlike and tranquil like an abandoned parade ground around her – that is to say, the people in the house have not only got used to her strange presence but have brought to maturity little by little the respectful and devoted opinion it has by now formed of their kinswoman.

In fact – since those who are superstitious are always realistic in their superstition – near Emilia, as she sits on one of the blood-red bricks in the little heap of ruins, a candle shines, as if under a sacred image. A humble, provisional candle, if you like, without any solemnity. Placed there to give a name and a meaning to what has happened. The old women of the house have got used to that new Emilia; they no longer spend their time pricking their ears suspiciously behind the white curtains but are in the courtyard; one of them keeps an eye on Emilia and another works – all with a special closeness to the phenomenon that is taking place in their house, to that mute Emilia, who is withdrawn and seems burnt by fever.

What also seems almost an everyday matter is the fact that from the big open door at the far end of the farmhouse, from the road which is white against the tender green of the fields and the poplars, a group of old men and women is advancing as if they were a group of pilgrims. They are obviously neighbours or people from that nearby village whose bell-tower appears beyond the rows of poplars, its maroon dome veined with red (and the ornaments, sumptuous and mean, of the centuries of the Counter-Reformation).

The new arrivals advance in a kind of procession until they come to a halt in a circle round Emilia. Among them – we notice her now because the others make a space around her – there is a middle-aged woman who looks old (with her black Sunday clothes, her silk stockings, her little open-work veil), who is holding in her arms a sick child, his suffering and humiliated face covered with little red sores or dry pustules.

Emilia seems not to see anything. And if her eyes at last come to rest on the sick child they do so as if he did not really exist but were merely an apparition. But she looks at him for a long time intently – as if she were discharging a duty somehow more bureaucratic than holy. Her participation in the ceremony in which she is the saint takes place in the same manner as the others accept her – almost like something codified, something that goes along with the actions of a motionless and blind sanctity. At last, absent-minded and almost ill-tempered, Emilia makes a slow sign of the cross in the direction of the child with the sores.

All the peasants' eyes are directed at the child in avid expectation of what in fact happens: the child begins to wave its arms and legs, looking at his mother and crying, and tries, by struggling to free himself from her embrace, to slip down her side until it puts a foot on the ground. Trembling, the mother, with her face full of divine joy that is already hallowed, lets him do what he wants and bends down to look at him. The child sets foot on the ground, keeping himself upright, swaying just a little; his face is tender and sweet as if newly washed; of the pustules which disfigured him not the slightest trace remains. Then all around, those present fall on their knees uttering loud cries of thanks and joy.

6

PIETRO'S COROLLARY

Pietro is alone in his room. He is sitting on the bed where the guest slept and is holding on his knees the big illustrated volume of contemporary painting which the two boys had looked at together one day.

He is searching in it, turning over the pages with attention, almost avidly, for something that truly interests him but which he has difficulty in finding because of his haste. It is the reproduction of the painting by Wyndham Lewis. He finds it and begins to look at it in a vaguely well-meaning way – as if he wished to interrogate it or as if his deciphering of it were the key to an oracle.

What reply can that poor reproduction of an Imagist painting from *c*. 1914 give?

Indeed, on the contrary it seems to have lost all that eloquent magic, that signifying tension, so splendidly over-charged with meaning, which had fascinated and almost moved Pietro the first time he had seen it with the guest.

Those coloured surfaces (so splendidly wasted as if the material on which they had been painted were sublime precisely because of its poverty: cardboard or cheap paper which easily turn yellow), those precise outlines, made with a single mark, so as to 'decompose' reality in accordance with a technique that was half cubist and half futurist but in truth neither truly cubist nor truly futurist – belonging, in short, to a civilization of 'decomposition' (but in reality something pure and orderly as in ancient crafts – simply to give an idea of how severe the avant-gardists of the early twentieth century were); all this seems faded, depreciated, disappointing, impoverished.

It is merely the case of something beautiful, elegant and poor: a small, useless enigma, since the meaning to which it referred is an historical meaning which seems to have no more value; and so it is there like a relic, without referents.

Yet Pietro pores over it as if he were searching for not only the historical meaning to which all these marks, which are so rigorous and precise, referred, but also the meaning which had been important to him and because of which that picture had been a revelation only a few weeks or a few months before.

7

NETTLES

The bells of all the villages of the Plain are ringing midday.
Thus the silence of the groves of poplars becomes festive – as
it should – and an acutely familiar feeling runs through all
things so that they all signify peace, regularity, the reassuring
value of ancient customs.

In the farmstead too, outside which Emilia is sitting
motionless on her bench, the midday peal brings an air of
peaceful cheerfulness. Inside, people eat and rest.

The door with its freshly washed curtains opens and, as if
in a kind of rite, the old women of the house come out,
faithfully followed by the two little children with adult
faces: they are bringing Emilia's dinner.

It is a nice dinner, carried on a tray – maybe a plastic one,
with a pattern of big flowers – unlike the dinners carried to
the men at work wrapped in knotted kerchiefs. There is
chicken, some sausages, fried chicory and a plate of fresh
tomatoes.

Proud of that dish of theirs, with a firm but not hasty step,
the women of the house carry the dinner to their saint; and
the children, ruddy and expressionless, follow, with their
daily interest, an operation so sweetly compounded of the
sacred and the familiar.

But this time adults and children find an unexpected
disappointment waiting for them.

Emilia glowers at the food offered to her on the elegant
tray and does not bat an eyelid, does not move a muscle.

117

Then, as people do with a deaf-mute, the women make expansive gestures as if to say: 'Look, here it is, look what platefuls, make an effort, come on, eat.' Nothing. In fact Emilia looks away from the food and stares at the sky. The women begin to be worried while a great sorrow seizes them. The eldest one, poor thing, with her child-like eyes full of tears, is more pressing than the others. It is precisely she – at her age she should be well aware that in the end nothing in this world is necessary and that to live is not a duty – who makes an effort to convince Emilia to eat, to take something at least in order to keep going – with the same arguments that people use to convince themselves to eat in order to survive – in the name of resignation and of the rights of life; she who has just suffered some bereavement and is weeping over it.

But Emilia simply does not allow herself to be convinced, whereas some neighbour in mourning, who is prepared to understand quickly about resignation and life's rights, would allow himself to be convinced: No – Emilia understands nothing. Who knows what goes on in that stubborn saintly head.

Since the women, with the old woman at their head, continue to insist passionately – before the bewildered eyes of the body and the little girl – Emilia with a bad tempered glance, her eyes filled with an overbearing expression born of pain, looks at her relatives one by one and at last, raising an arm slowly, points to something beside the heap of rubble and red bricks. It is a clump of nettles.

8

MORE NETTLES

The two children from the farmhouse (there are only two of them while there are at least a dozen old folk and the only man still fairly young is their coarse father) are on the grass in front of the house, intent on a task which seems more than ever like the one laid on the children in the fairytale.

They are gathering nettles.

Wrapped up in their clothes – those of up-to-date peasants and already almost the same as those of the bourgeoisie – they are gathering nettles in silence, diligently. Only the little girl from time to time wails a little because the nettles sting her.

The boy holds the pot in his hand. And it is already almost full. They are bending over the grass so washed by recent rains as to look like the grass in books of fairytales. And round about, almost making one feel giddy because of their green, there stretch the meadows surrounded by the regular files of poplars, shining through one another.

In the midst of all this green – glowing as if in the south or in the heart of Africa and yet pale, of a perfect purity – the reddish colour of the farmstead shines with its strange archaic shapes rendered extravagant by their strict functionalism – like a barracks with its sentry-boxes, its astronomical observatories, its abandoned bastions and its purely decorative towers.

They have no sooner filled their pot than the two children, comical and careful, re-enter the courtyard of the farmstead through the big round gateway.

119

And there at the other end, against her old crumbling wall, which is pink and reddish, is Emilia in her black jumper, motionless on her bench.

The two children go over until they are in front of her. At a proper distance they stop and with habitual gestures – because evidently they have been carrying out this task for a long time – put down the earthenware pot full of nettles and busy themselves lighting with fire in a kind of little fireplace made from some of the old red bricks from the heap of rubble, which is already full of ashes from previous regular kindlings.

The fire flames up, sweet and familiar and the nettles in the pot begin to cook. In a few minutes they are ready and steaming.

Some of the old women from the house come, out of habit – but disappointed and sad – to be present at the meal, keeping a little to one side with a devout air.

Another group of old peasant women arrives through the big gate murmuring the rosary. Murmuring in this way they come and so too form a circle round the corner which the saint has chosen as the site of her solitude.

Then the two children, confused by shyness (they also hold a wooden spoon which has emerged from the little girl's coat), bring Emily her green soup to eat.

Emilia glowers at them, lost in the rigour of her sanctity. But there is something strange about her – indeed something extraordinary – and there is no doubt that is a case of something with a miraculous aura about it. But it is difficult to say how far it is proper for a saint (if Emilia is a saint) . . .

Eating nettles continually and exclusively has turned her hair green – her eyelashes, her eyebrows and the hair of her head. Her skin too is slightly greenish, especially round the eyes.

But what is most impressive of all is her head: her permanent wave is now undone, her hair drawn tight over her brow and curling thick, full and singed behind her ears. The two gold dots of her ear-rings for first communion shine in her ear-lobes.

The nettle-green of that permanent wave, which is typical of a peasant servant-girl, is not calculated to confer the dignity due to her silence and her injured saintly solitude. And in fact the old women of the house look at her worried and sighing – accomplices brought together by this kind of misfortune (or rather destiny) in the face of which they are powerless.

But Emilia, who has withdrawn elsewhere with sullen eyes that look at nothing, eats with slow spoonfuls the green fare of her scandalous penance.

9

VOCATION AND SKILLS

Pietro is bending over some white sheets of paper. He is
drawing. He is so keen and intent on drawing (he is drawing a
head which resembles – certainly crudely – that of the guest)
that he forgets he is alone and talks out loud, commenting on
and criticizing what he is doing.

He is disgusted with it – the disappointment and displeasure
his drawings cause him is like a pang which disfigures his
feaures and makes his voice hoarse.

In the end he tears up, crumples and throws away the sheet
of paper on which he is drawing.

*

Pietro is still drawing – but he has had a bigger table,
covered with paper and pencils, brought into his room.

But now that he is better organized he is not however
more pleased with what he manages to do.

He begins a new sheet of paper, immaculate – as if seized
by an inspiration that is almost joyful in its boyish ferocity.
But then, as the drawing little by little takes shape (it is still
the guest's head) disgust and anger take the place of hope and
good intentions. And he continues to talk out loud to himself
(with the hoarse, tuneless and lamenting voice, precisely the
one with which one speaks without dignity when one is
alone). He passes judgement on his errors with pitiless
contempt, makes sardonic comments, shouts out 'Shit' and

ends up by insulting himself, calling himself an idiot, impotent, a turd.

Pietro is still bending over to draw. But this time in the garden on a huge piece of paper (made up of various sheets pasted on to plywood) which certainly would not have fitted into his room. In fact it takes up a whole piece of the lawn.

Pietro is no longer drawing with a pencil but with a large brush, leaning over that sheet of paper like someone laying paving stones.

But he is still complaining bitterly to himself, muttering ungraciously to himself that that drawing is not like him, is not like him, will never be like him – and even if it is going to be like him the result will be horrible and absurd – that the other found him in the void (floundering like this with a brush in his hand) and will leave him in the void. Poor new Emilia, who comes bringing him a Coca-Cola, catches him in the full flow of his monologue. And, in the manner of a servant girl, listens to her master's bold plans for his future: some way of making it his own, of becoming an author, an artist, a creator. But after these bold assurances (given to the servant who adores him) there quickly follow the bitter ironies of doubt, the cold ruminations of distress.

To draw, to paint, to become an author – this after all is merely to put oneself on show, to risk coming into contact with a world that must learn everything about the person who presents himself and learns it without any regard for him – almost as if he were predestined, a messenger from heaven; and so it knows nothing of his solitude, thinks he is already formed to live publicly, in a place where (justly in this case) there is no pity.

And what humiliating tests an artist must go through! What a wretched thing this brush is, with its little games of contours, of blobs, of smudges on a piece of gummed paper. What poor instruments, what wretched means one has to use! What a childish thing is this technique, this unavoidable practical and manual moment, this business of leaning like students over a piece of paper, and making marks on it, making marks carefully, always as if it were the first time, with one's tongue sticking out, with one's eyes excited and a terrible sense of shame flooding the whole body which is used like a dummy.

*

Still hunched over the sheets of paper, Pietro is trying out new techniques to try to overcome the shame of normal techniques.

Around him he has, in a state of disorder, jumbled together, oil paints, watercolours, tempera, pastels; but what is most impressive is the presence of a heap of materials, *all of them transparent*: cellophane, thick and thin; tissue paper; gauzes; pieces of glass, above all pieces of glass.

While trying out these new techniques – as alone in that garden as a dog – Pietro has naturally not lost the habit of talking, of passing judgment, of complaining, of commenting to himself on what he is doing. What he is still doing over and over again disgusts him. With a brush he sketches on the cardboard base the shape of a head (still the head of the guest?), then he sticks on the cardboard thus marked (the gum is yellowish and he does not worry about the blobs of still fresh oil) a veil of gauze and with a brush dipped in a turquoise blue, he makes two patches of colour where presumably the eyes should be; then once more, still playing no heed to possible blots, he places over the cardboard and the veil of gauze a large piece of glass; and here with a brush dipped in light sepia he traces around the blue patches on the gauze (which show through the glass) and within the black background of the cardboard (which shows through the glass and the gauze) the circles of the eyes.

He laughs and laughs. He laughs at the resulting blobs – bitter, disgusted with himself, sincerely amused by his clumsiness, overexcited and disappointed.

*

There is a great heap of drawings and pictures in Pietro's little room (he has gone back to small dimensions and so has come inside again). Inspired, mad, rapt, the boy bends over his material, kneeling, which this time is supported on a kind of big lectern (and since that material is still transparent it would be possible to look at Pietro through the picture he is painting). Having finished painting the first glass in silence, Pietro places the second on the first glass making the monochrome of the second shine through onto the first (monochrome) picture.

Pietro's movements as he carries out these operations are mechanical and inspired; and his voice which tirelessly comments on them has lost all colour; low, scarcely perceptible, it exactly follows these movements.

New techniques – they must be unrecognizable ones – have to be invented which resemble no other previous operation. To avoid in this way puerility and the ridiculous. To construct a world of one's own with which no comparisons are possible. For which no criteria exist. The criteria must be new – like the technique. No one must see that the author is worthless, that he is an abnormal, inferior being, like a worm writhing in order to survive. No one must catch him out being naïve. Everything must present itself as perfect, based on *unknown rules* and therefore impossible to judge. Like a madman, yes, like a madman. Glass on glass because Pietro is incapable of making corrections – but no one must notice this. A mark painted on a piece of glass corrects, without dirtying it, a mark painted beforehand on another piece of glass. But everyone must think that this is not a case of the expedient of someone lacking in skill, of someone who is *impotent* – but that on the contrary it is a case of a sure, undaunted decision that is haughty and almost overweening: a newly invented and already irreplacable technique. That is to say, cellophane or gauze glued onto glass and entirely transparent on top of some marks which by chance, have come off well on a piece of cardboard after a thousand painful attempts and thousands of other pieces of cardboard torn up.

No one must know that a mark works well by chance. By chance and trembling – and that the moment a mark has appeared which, by miracle, has come off well, one has at once to protect it and cherish it in a safe place. But no one, no one must be aware of this. The author is a poor trembling idiot. A bit of a whore. He lives in the midst of chance and risk, as disgraced as a child. He has reduced his life to the ridiculous melancholy of someone who lives degraded by the sense of being something forever lost.

*

Transformed in his looks – that is to say, having become pale, thin, with long hair and the first hairs on his callow cheeks unpleasantly black along his sideburns – and dressed too in a different, neglected, dirty way – Pietro is about to leave home. He says goodbye in silence to his mother Lucia and his father Paolo and he goes out. The new Emilia with big damp and pitiful eyes makes to take his luggage and help him. But Pietro gets there before her, grasps his luggage, his bag and without turning round goes out of the house.

He walks straight down the usual road in front of his house, the one down which the guest had disappeared. He too disappears down it, unaware of it, ploughing his way through its sad, hateful, withdrawn silence.

*

Pietro (in his new studio (which is certainly in the centre of town) is intent on a newly finished painting. It is simply a surface painted blue (the same blue with which the guest's eyes have usually been painted). It is the blue that is his memory. But the blue alone evidently is not enough. The blue is only a part. Who can give Pietro the right to carry out such a mutilation? What ideologies, he asked himself, suffice to justify it? So were not the first miserable attempts at true portraits better? Ah! the truth is this: that both the surfaces done solely in blue and the realistic portraits, are merely useless and ridiculous pretexts. And he does not paint to express himself but probably only to tell everyone of his impotence.

Seized by a ferocious impulse of hatred – or else with the slightly vulgar calm of someone who has weighed things up – from his squatting position in front of his picture he stands up straight, unbutton his trousers and pisses on it.

10

'YES, OF COURSE, WHAT DO YOUNG
PEOPLE DO . . .?'

Yes, of course, what do young people do, intelligent
people from well-off families, if not
talk about literature and painting?
Maybe even with friends from lower down the social
    scale –
a little cruder but also more plagued
by ambition. Talk about literature and painting,
vulgar and factious, ready to turn everything
    upside-down,
already beginning to warm with their young bottoms
café chairs already warmed by the bottoms of the
    hermetic poets?[1]
Or else walking about (that is tramping over the divine
    pavements
of the old part of the city, like soldiers or whores)
subversive types sick with bourgeois snobbery –
even with all their sincerity, their idealism,
their vocation to action: the painful shadow, that is,
of Yesenin or Simone Weil in their souls?
But let's see: whether they come sweating
from little flats with sad
blankets burnt by the iron or cupboards

[1] The school of poetry, non-rhetorical and closed, that included Montale,
Ungaretti and Quasimodo (Tr.).

costing their secretly loved fathers a few thousand lire –
whether instead they come from houses surrounded
by the halo of wealth, with almost celestial habits
of servants and tradesmen – all the young men of letters
are grimy, have a pallor of the elderly,
if not of the old, their graceful qualities are already
    chipped;
they have an irresistable vocation for heavy meals
and woollen clothes, they tend to have evil-smelling
illnesses – of the teeth or the intestines –
they have problems about shitting: in short are petty
    bourgeois
like their magistrate brothers or businessmen uncles.
It is one big family lacking in any sort of love.
Every so often an Adorable Person turns up
in this family. But it is odd:
he too, like the others, the shitty ones,
invokes (since the beginning of the last century and,
after a brief interruption between 1945–1955,
up to the present day) an exterminating God:
exterminator of himself and of his social class. I too
    invoke him!
And once before this invocation has been listened to.
Youths draped in Sioux shawls, bogus youths from
    Turin
already stamped with blue loden, destroyers of
    grammars,
castrato boarding-school students who pass up meals at
    Monza,
new political ignoramuses in furs who love the
    Brandenburg
Concertos as if they had discovered an antibourgeois
formula which makes them look around furiously,

gently morose democrats convinced that only
true democracy destroys the false; little blond
anarchists who, in perfectly good faith, confuse
dynamite with their own sperm (going about
with big guitars through streets
as false as stage-sets in mangy packs); naughty little
    boys
from the universities who go and occupy the Senate
    House
demanding Power instead of renouncing it once and for
    all;
guerillas who, with their females at their side,
have decided that the Blacks are like the Whites
(but perhaps the Whites not also like the Blacks); all of
    them
merely preparing the way
of the new exterminating God
stamped, innocently, with a hooked cross;
yet they will be the first to enter a gas-chamber
with real diseases upon them and real rags. And is that
    not
what they rightly want?
Do they not want the destruction – the most terrible
    possible
of themselves and the social class to which they belong?
I with my little prick, all skin and hair
always, of course, able to do its duty, although
    humiliated
forever by a centaur's prick, heavy and divine,
immense and in proportion, tender and powerful;
I who wander in the recesses of moralizing and
    sentimentality
to fight with both, seeking their alienation

(an alienated orality, an alienated sentimentality,
in the place of the real ones; with simulated fits of
    inspiration
and therefore still more incredible than authentic ones
destined to ridicule as is the bourgeois custom);
I find myself, in short, in a mechanism
which has always worked in the same way.
The Bourgeoisie is clear and adores reason;
and yet because of its own bad conscience
it works away to punish and destroy itself: so appointing
    as
delegates for its own destruction,
none other than its degenerate children who
(some of them idiotically maintaining
a useless bourgeois dignity as men-of-letters,
independent or downright reactionary and servile; some
    instead
going right on to the end and losing themselves)
obey that obscure mandate.
And they begin to invoke the above-mentioned God.
Hitler arrives and the Bourgeoisie is happy.
It dies, tortured, by its own hand.
It punishes itself by the hand of a hero of its own, from
    its own guilts.
What do the young people of 1968 talk of – with their
    barbaric
hair and Edwardian clothes, vaguely militaristic in style,
which cover members as unhappy as my own –
if not of literature and painting? And what does this
mean if not to invoke from the darkest recess
of the petty bourgeoisie the exterminating God
to strike them once more
for crimes still greater than those that ripened in 1938?

Only we bourgeois know that we are gangsters
and instead the young extremists, unseating Marx and
    dressing
themselves in the Flea Market, merely shout
like generals and people with degrees against generals
    and
people with degrees.
It is civil war.
Those who die of consumption,
dressed like moujiks, not yet sixteen,
are perhaps the only ones to be right.
The others tear each other to pieces.

11

IN WHICH IT IS DESCRIBED HOW
MASTER PIETRO ENDS UP BY LOSING
OR BETRAYING GOD

Pietro is in the middle of his big room with his eyes shut – but furiously shut and therefore with wrinkles all round them and his mouth half-open in a grimace of rage.

Thus, with his eyes shut, he moves about in the milky light of his big rich room, which is that of a rebellious painter. Groping and feeling at things, he goes towards a wall where unpainted canvases are leaning, takes one and then another; choses a canvas the dimensions of which seem to him to be right for the operation he is carrying out.

Tottering, he carries the canvas to the centre of the room and lays it on the ground. Then, still blind, still obstinately blind, he goes towards another corner of the big room. The task is now much more complicated and two or three times he runs the risk of falling: he makes a choice from among the paints. His hand passes gropingly over the watercolours, the oils, the varnishes; at last it reaches the place he is looking for: a heap of tins. He mixes them up – as if he were mixing cards or shaking dice to help chance – then he chooses a tin. It is shut. So he has to open it. He goes towards the table like a drunkard; but he has lost his sense of direction and he has trouble in finding it. Now he has to find a drawer and in the drawer he has to find an instrument with which to open the tin. Here is a screwdriver. With it, he clumsily makes a hole in the tin. Now it is a question of once more reaching the picture left on the floor in the centre of the large room. At first Pietro looks for it with the tips of his feet with which, step by step, he is exploring things around him. Then he bends down and walks, almost brushing against the floor, on all fours – but with difficulty because he has to hold the tin with one hand. At last he stumbles on the canvas stretched out on the ground. He touches it triumphantly. Feeling it with the palm of his hand, he tries to find the centre, more or less. He holds the tin above the centre of the picture then very gradually he stands upright, trying to keep the tin always on the same axis. When he is on his feet, with a rapid gesture he turns the tin upside-down and lets a little of its liquid fall haphazardly on the centre of the picture. The patch – it is blue – spreads over it, throwing out little splashes. Then Pietro sets the tin on the ground and takes hold of the picture painted in this way. Still swaying like a drunk man and not heeding that the liquid is dripping, he goes in search of an empty wall with a nail in it, certainly put there beforehand, and there he hangs the picture. But he still does not open his eyes to look at it; instead with his eyes still shut and almost with his face distended and swollen by a smile of deep and ferocious satisfaction, he goes back towards the centre of his empty room . . .

12

LUCIA'S COROLLARY

Lucia is finishing making up or doing her hair in front of the mirror where this daily ritual is carried out. But there is no doubt that she is far away. In fact when, with due calm and care, she has finished combing her hair which – like some really rich ladies and some truly aristocratic ones – she wears in an old-fashioned cut with waves that come down almost covering her eyes to produce a touch of refinement that is slightly girlish and mannerist, and a little whorish – she sadly throws the comb onto the table among her precious toilet things.

She gets up full of that sadness. Then she sighs and almost with a touch of irony (absurd in her face – that of a people's heroine) which in an illusory way stretches her lineaments, she slips on her overcoat or a fur-coat and goes out.

Waiting for her in the road in front of the house is her car. She gets in with that calm of hers which is mixed with frenzy, puts it in gear and drives off.

She too loses herself down the silent street where the guest was lost; she too is swallowed up by that desolate and arrogant stage-set of houses of the rich for whom it is a duty to give no sign of life.

The set alone remains – the index of an unreality which, in concrete terms, takes the form of a district of the dead, whose stones, whose cement, whose trees are a spectacle, motionless under the sun, which by its mere presence causes pain and offence.

*

The world through which a lady's car can pass when the goals are no longer those foreseen and fixed by a habit that cannot be broken but are those which sin maps out, trusting to chance, is – in spite of the reversal of the situation – the most prosaic, sad and everyday one.

So Lucia, numb and desperate, explores the city in search of something which undoubtedly she will succeed in finding in the end but which for so long, perhaps even for the whole day, seems an impossible miracle.

She is at fault (she is driving about looking for a miracle to happen while everyone is busy with the enchanting miseries of everyday); but her fault is the fruit of a right she believes to be hers.

So almost haughtily (in so far as this is allowed her by the sweetness of her face – that of a Lombardy girl educated in piety, in respect and in an innocent kind of hypocrisy) she represses every anxiety, every shame, every voice of good sense; giving herself over to her search with the obstinacy of a scientist or of a famished animal writhing in silence.

What part of the city is this? Of the great industrial metropolis where duty and work are like a climate which prevents miracles from flowering? Is it on the outskirts on the way to the Plain or on the way to Switzerland? On the way to Cosenza or on the way to Venice? In what industrial zone with its factories as silent as churches or schools during the hours of work?

Since this is the moment when the miracle happens, the spot is semi-deserted, peaceful, with few passers-by and a sun radiant with good fortune even if it is so weak. The shelter rises empty on the pavement and under this shelter is the boy with the light eyes. He is waiting for his tram without anxiety, with dignity; and solitude, instead of urging him to assume poses on laziness or cheekiness, rather encloses him in a kind of grace that is more compact and gentle.

He is tall, with a movingly pronounced profile, the gauche and thick hair of a simple boy who doesn't comb it, dark skin and a tall body which nevertheless, because of its good proportions, does not seem so and which gives to his youth a virile and solid look (not that of an athlete but rather that of a peasant).

Lucia stops the car a little beyond the shelter; but a sudden shyness immobilizes her – so much that she does not even have the courage to look round towards him; very slowly she takes out a cigarette with her eyes fixed on empty space and murmurs to herself the bitter thoughts that agitate her and give her that desperate calm, and very nearly the decision to give up . . .

She stays there – bent over – with the cigarette which has gone out between her lips, with an icy and bitter smile. Mechanically she starts up the car but without driving off.

When (as if by chance!) she turns her head towards the pavement, she sees the boy there nearby, close to her. Perhaps he is a university student – one of those from a poor family who come from the provinces. Otherwise how would he have had the courage to come forward – with a woman like her, so beautiful, so unfriendly, so protected by her obvious social privilege – and actually smile to her with timid and intelligent complicity?

So Lucia does not need to ask him for a light – that damnable request that did not come to her lips: she only needed to smile to him very slightly, making a shy gesture which indicates that her cigarette has gone out and the consequent natural need . . .

But the boy – with that smile of his which now has a

decidedly humorous air that no longer leaves doubts as to his social origins and his culture, which is that of a university student at least – opens his arms with a nice comical gesture of disappointment giving her to understand that he does not smoke.

But then he does something really audacious (the audacious acts of those who are healthily timid – timid, perhaps, only because of the humble nature of their lives) and running with a naïve gait like a happy dog, catches up with a passer-by, asks him for matches, comes back, lights Lucia's cigarette, returns the matches to the passer-by and comes back once more . . . Yes, that's what he must be: a student from a petty-bourgeois family or a working-class family in the provinces still bearing – it cannot be eliminated – with grace the humility and the roughness, in short the marks of poverty.

Lucia does not even know how and why and with what gesture of complicit comradeship and what absolutely unconscious lack of prejudice she leans over and opens the door: the boy slips in quickly, happily, accepting the adventure as something right, absolute and entirely capable of giving happiness.

*

The house where the boy lives is precisely the kind that students manage to find who come from the provinces to study at the university. It is a house that is neither old nor new but certainly very sad, lost in the midst of a cluster of houses, neither old nor new, which stand among a group of very new houses, shining with glass and metal – recent and triumphant works of neo-capitalism – and another little group (a divine one) of old houses from the nineteenth century, if not older, with the amazing proportions of their grey walls, with their cornices, their entrances, their old stables; beautiful as churches. This entire district is almost in the country, across a footbridge which is suspended in the distance like a whiteish apparition against the greyish haze – and almost among the great, infinite lines of poplars which begin immediately beyond a canal with old stone embankments.

The car is left in a line of other cars along the chipped pavement of the sad houses which are neither old nor new; and Lucia and the boy go into one of those sad entrances.

The stairs are half-dark; one cannot but look at them and one cannot but feel an intense pain when looking at them.

The boy goes upstairs impatiently; there is no doubt that, had it depended on him, he would have taken four steps at a time and in an instant would have been at the top of those sad stairs, which are collapsing towards the top in a smell of cabbage and old wet clothes.

They arrive in front of the little door of the flat, somehow or other.

In the room there is a small bed (tidily made) and it is there that, without looking round, the couple go and lie down, almost falling, beginning to attempt to exhaust their exhaustible yearning. They stay there a long time – until he gets up suddenly, as if frightened for some unexpected reason (so that Lucia is really frightened) and takes off his jacket, then he leans down to kiss her; but he gets up at once, suddenly again, to take off his shirt (a more complicated business which therefore requires a few shy smiles); he bends down to kiss her again; then he stands up again, this time to take off his T-shirt in haste and to unbutton his trousers. Like this he lies down on her once more and begins to kiss her anew. But suddenly – and again unexpectedly – he collapses on top of her as if he had fallen asleep, hiding his face between her shoulder and her cheek.

Lucia respects this first and premature fatigue (certainly due to all that youth he finds he is burdened with and which is like a gift to be thrown away), and takes the opportunity to look at him and to look around her. Of him she sees only a little ruffled hair and a burning ear; but the glance that explores the room discovers everything there is there sadly evident: poverty, thrift, sadness, commonsense.

On the floor are the boy's clothes newly discarded – like the footprints of someone who has just passed by and who has suddenly disappeared into the distance.

But no, he is still there, present: he begins to move again, to caress her, to give those overbearing kisses of his but ones that are too fresh, too innocent; almost as if he wished merely to satisfy an appetite unfamiliar to himself or else as though he were madly – and without knowing it – following rules dictated by a habit that pre-exists him and of which he is a simple slave, faithful and happy.

13

IN WHICH IT IS DESCRIBED HOW LUCIA ALSO
ENDS UP BY LOSING OR BETRAYING GOD

It seems incredible that the night can be so lifeless and so full
of the lifeless desire to be so.

Yet, who knows how, at the bottom of the abyss of the
mist clinging to the earth – beyond the vapours that drift
over the roofs and the tops of the poplars – beyond the torn
low bank of cloud and, finally, beyond the boundlessly high
clouds – the guarantees perhaps of fine weather the next day,
one glimpses a sliver of moon as thin as a slice of lemon or
pumpkin: a moon that is setting and going away, unobserved
and defeated.

A little of that atrociously melancholy moonlight enters
the room where Lucia is lying with her eyes open on the small
tumbled bed.

As he sleeps in the unconsciousness of his sleep which is full
of rights, of an almost offensive innocence, the boy has taken
up all the bed with his body, thus pushing Lucia to the edge
where certainly, even if she had the wish to, she would not be
able to fall asleep again. To wake up is for her to find herself
deep in a state of intense stupor – and of pain just as incurable
as the dying light of that moon which announces the day.

The objects in the room stand out vividly and one by one
are a source of pity and shame: the little desk with the waxy
cloth under the window, the two or three chairs, the little
shelves on the wall with their reading light (probably all
bought secondhand); the little table with the big, severe

books for study and the text books, the wardrobe which doubtlessly contains the basic necessities to dress oneself (things certainly looked after with a care the thought of which brings a pang), the tawdry paper on the walls, the reproductions of two or three famous paintings framed with a strip of cardboard and above the bed, naturally, a plaster Madonna, white and blue, of the kind one sees in kitchens.

Lucia gets up like a ghost – without having (as is obvious) come to any decision. Perhaps out of pure love or perhaps only to go to the window to look at the source of that atrocious light which illuminates the room.

Instead she stands beside the bed and looks at the boy's clothes scattered on the floor.

They have remained as he threw them down the evening before (but how many hours have passed?), undressing in haste as boys do who are so uncritical of their clumsy rights. And now they are like the skin of an animal which has left its traces here, the signs of its passage across the earth, and has gone for ever.

The lifelike quality of the clothes, so poor and prosaic, is in contrast, an absurd one, with the distance their owner has travelled in his dreams: the trousers crumpled, with the buttons at the crotch undone, open on the floor in all their unconscious naïveté; the underpants perhaps not entirely spotless with their sad signs of life; the T-shirt which on the other hand looks splendid, struck by the moonlight which this time is serene; the shoes dramatically thrown upside down in all that peace, the nice thick woollen jumper of a colour that is not lively but yet mysteriously youthful . . . But his socks the boy has not taken off; they are still on the feet of his naked body.

He is sleeping on his side – foetus-like – with his arms

stretched down and close together (between his thighs against his crotch).

Lucia looks at him like a survivor: his innocence, which is so blind, gives her pain; the breathing in his sleep, which is too regular and a little dirty, the beauty of his face made sordid and inadequate by sweat and pallor and perhaps a certain indistinct smell, which comes from all over him (perhaps from those socks not removed from his feet), disgust her, it is clear, a disgust increased by the inoffensive nature and unconsciousness of the one who is causing it and who is so stupidly overcome by bodily needs. It is a disgust that is almost hate for him – a real desire to strike him, to insult him, with indignation and contempt, so that he understands once and for all that a man must never go off into sleep, must not give in, must not die!

But yet Lucia cannot overcome a certain tenderness, the final and definitive feeling which she will have as she steathily leaves; she is already dressing, has already slipped on her skirt, when she approaches him, caressing once more that naked body whose muscles have been loosened, have become soft, ignorant flesh. And she makes her way down his chest, as broad and nice as a piazza, down over the stomach divided by its two symmetrical muscles (as in statues) over the belly still without a trace of fat, but already almost too virile, with a thin shadow of hair going up to the navel, until she touches his penis, which is innocent of anything except the misery of the flesh.

Then Lucia finishes dressing, very quietly, overcome once more by a pain that has no name and certainly no cure.

She takes her things and leaves the room not even very furtively and in silence.

*

The district where the boy lives is left behind; the public lights (a lamp in front of the door of each of the sad little blocks) go out. Day appears, mangy, moonless and with the white bank of cloud everywhere the same.

Along the canal with the stone banks, accompanied by a long border of grass, here is the road that runs to the centre.

Resigned people on the way to work are already there; some on foot making for the tram stop; some on motor bikes or sad old scooters; the cars are already going past one after another, disturbing, the ferocious six-litre jobs of six in the morning.

But there, on the other side of the street, leaning against a little bridge that crosses the canal, are two figures with that special air that distinguishes them from everything else like the natural privilege of another race: youth.

Lucia scarcely notices them while another car crosses in front of her. They raise their hands, confident and over-weening, asking without any kind of politeness the favour of a lift.

Lucia goes on for another four hundred metres, then she slows down and, deciding desperately to make a dangerous turn, goes back to the threats of the drivers of the little cars which are coming up in swarms. The couple are not at all surprised: they give the hitch-hikers' questioning and uncommitted signal and when Lucia slows down and stops they run up and, having exchanged the few barely necessary words, climb in.

The boy sitting next to her has blue eyes. He sits with his legs apart, upright, like certain statues in the old peasant churches, like the Homeric kings; but it is probably only the satisfaction of being seated in a car of such horse-power.

The one in the back has a foxy and detached air; perhaps because of the two he is the second or inferior one (either

144

owing to age or something else) and so he watches events the course of which is up to the other, his friend, and he gives himself over, a little ironically, to looking on sympathetically.

But the other, for the time being, is prey to a strange, stubborn feeling of distraction; he is caught up in watching the road, in following its course. Almost automatically he unbuttons his coat, looking ahead, correct and distant: his two big innocent thighs stick out wrapped in the cloth (it is too light) of his trousers – summer ones (in spite of the time of day and the almost wintry cold).

Lucia, who is equally absent-minded, takes her right hand from the wheel, passes it through her ruffled hair (for an instant her face is also covered; and her angry, wax-cold indifference, for that moment, melts into a grimace of pain or terror); then she lets her hand fall as if from fatigue, from early morning boredom, not on the wheel but on the edge of her seat, leaving it there, inert.

The boy who has always been looking ahead – and so how did he manage to notice? – very slowly brings his hand, the strong hand of a worker or a criminal, close to hers and after having barely touched it with his little finger seizes it; with a tug he brings it over to his open thigh covered by the almost transparent material, and then with a second tug to his crotch.

The car runs along the shining asphalt of a road that loses itself somewhere or other.

To the right there is a track with two ancient ruts from carts and in the middle a ridge of dirty grass which pushes its way through the irrigation channels.

Almost mechanically, Lucia turns off and drives along the little road by a huge and trembling row of poplars where there appears, miraculously, an old abandoned hay-shed a little beyond a ditch full of water. To get there, there is a bridge made of two rotten beams.

Lucia and the boy get out of the car, cross the little bridge, pass the red and grey walls of the hay-shed through grass which is dripping with dew or with rain fallen in the night.

The boy pushes her against the wall and without even embracing her or kissing her begins to undo his trouser-belt.

They have quickly finished making love – the boy needed only a few minutes (he has just got out of bed full of youthful sleep and brimming with sperm which needed almost nothing to release it). Fastening his belt he goes off with sarcely a timid glance at Lucia (but of a timidity without embarrassment).

He disappears round the corner and Lucia lingers to adjust herself while the grimace of pain or rather of terror comes back to distort her sweet, ravaged face.

Behind her, from round the corner of the low wall, the other boy appears with his light and almost too elegant coat, the collar up and underneath old jeans. Only at this moment does Lucia realize the tacit bargain and the fact that her will participates in it. The new boy *does not have blue eyes* and is not beautiful like the other, he is common and somewhat unpleasant. Lucia moves away from the wall and makes as if to leave, revolting against the violence and the silence of that unformulated bargain; still in the grip of the thought – a true one – that this boy does not interest, does not please her. But he holds her back with one hand against the wall – already so certain of having overwhelmed her that he does not lose his childlike sweetness and the openness of someone who basically is asking a favour: the weight of his hand on her shoulder and the gesture of the other hand which is already on his crotch – of a young mature father.

146

*

Lucia leaves the two boys in the piazza of a village surrounded by factories and poplars. They get out and say goodbye. Then they go off excitedly at a quick pace towards their morning occupations in this place which their life knows well. Lucia starts the car and sets off again towards the countryside.

She is suddenly in the midst of irrigation canals and clumps of poplars. The morning is turning fine and the green is shining sadly and festively.

A river appears, caught between the two dark banks, green with a green from the abyss polished like brass. Then a clump of poplars, thick and with infinitely long regular lines which lose themselves down there where the sun triumphs sadly.

Then the shallow valleys appear which open up the horizon almost up to the Po and in the centre, among lonely square formations of poplars, irrigation channels so discoloured that they seem almost white, as mysterious as oriental rice paddies.

The roads point in the direction of these visions. And one follows the other as if in a sparse labyrinth. To turn to the right is the same as to turn to the left: to make for the mountains, which are shimmering as white as in a dream, is the same as to make for the depression of the Po which seems real, it is true, downright realistic but profoundly alien like a peasant world of long past and forgotten times.

Thus Lucia, unable to find the road to take her home, goes round that elegaic labyrinth which is so disgustingly sad in spite of the splendour of the green. Sometimes she turns and goes back, in the very middle of a narrow tarred road which, whether ahead or behind her, is perfectly identical; at other

147

times, after making for a crossroad to the right, she suddenly changes her mind and drives to the left. To lose herself among the rows of poplars, blind with their ancient, never resolved sylvan mystery.

Lucia's disorientation, depicted on her face which looks as if it has turned to glass, hides a single iron determination. But what? Perhaps it is only obstinacy, a refusal. A 'no' said to a truth however humble, rare and desperate.

She goes down a road like the others (perhaps one she has already travelled down), then at a crossroads, decisively this time, goes to the right, (it has, on this side and that, the amphitheatres of poplars which are rendered uneven by the bed of a river dirty from the waste of the factories, perhaps the Lambro); she arrives at a track with its usual green ridge in the middle. Here she stops, caught and enchanted by an apparition which does not astonish her, does not cheer her but simply absorbs her, *plunging her into a rapid series of calculations both precise and inspired.*

The result of this meditation is that Lucia gets out of the car and goes on foot towards the vision that has stopped her in her drive which is full of mad changes of direction.

It is a solitary chapel in the midst of an expanse of channels and poplars: a whiteish-yellowish chapel, small, elegant – sprung certainly from the still baroque head of some provincial artist, living at the height of neo-classicism; so absurd and perfect with its neat eighteenth century orna-mentation much more like blazons of the nobility than any symbol of faith.

It is set down, absolutely alone and isolated in the midst of the countryside.

The small broken door, although recently remade by the old faithful believers of the nineteenth century, stands ajar; and with a creak opens at Lucia's timid push.

The interior is all nineteenth century – sad, to tell the truth, stupid and bigoted. But the rows of benches, broken and unused like the door, and a single tiny confessional in a state of collapse, precisely because left in that totally abandoned state, do not lack the melancholy of the ancient, terrible religion beyond whose bounds the miserable brothers have passed and have been lost along with the light of their suns.

In the little apse above the empty, dusty altar there is painted a crucifixion – certainly the work of a poor romantic artist, the crude and mannered copyist of Renaissance machinery now good only for the common people; so that the Christ hanging on the cross looks like a spiritual youngster, a little stupid and ambiguous – but still fairly virile with two blue eyes full of what should be Divine Mercy.

We shall not enter Lucia's consciousness. Having made the sign of the cross she remained motionless beside the door; there is no other expression in her than that due to the liquid black blotch of her eyes, staring and lost.

It is towards that Christ that she is attracted, leaving his thin body there near the door like a cast-off skin returning to its old life.

14

LEVITATION

The bench against the chipped wall of the farmstead is empty. Emilia is no longer there.

Today she is to be found higher up – but not at one of the little windows, all of them shut, of the first floor nor at one of the little unglazed one in the granary. She is actually above the cornice, above the roof.

In short Emilia *is suspended in the sky*. And she stays there for no reason with her arms outspread.

Perhaps she has already been there for hours; high up, like a weather balloon or a hanged woman, against the bank of grey cloud through which – it is already almost evening – an absurd blue sky peeps out.

Down below in the courtyard there is, in fact, a big crowd looking up into the air, not knowing what to say, what to do, alienated and maddened by this novelty. Only the small boy with the nettles, a little relative of the saint suspended above the roof, perhaps because he is a child and so more happy than astonished, gets the idea to do something: he runs towards the little tower of the farmstead where, in an arch against the sky, an old bell dangles; he grabs the rope and begins to ring the bell; to ring it.

At that harsh and unsettling sound the extraordinary scene that is taking place in the farmstead acquires a more human meaning and people somehow or other are able to rediscover the gestures and actions required in such cases, recognizing before their own eyes the ancient and well-known presence of God.

Some stand and look at their feet, some fall on their knees, some are silent, some pray, some are dumbfounded and some are moved to tears. The stupefying presence of that little black figure hanging above the edge of the roof against a giddy sky, which is full of the melancholy sunset clouds edged with light, is a vision that cannot satisfy and exhaust the mad happiness with which it fills them.

Besides, one has to admit, to be witnesses of something of the kind is not an everyday matter. Now no one would be able to say what the shadows would bring, which, as in every evening, are slowly and severely coming from the sky.

15

AN INVESTIGATION INTO SAINTHOOD

At this point the reader has to undertake a difficult and perhaps unpleasant operation – that of turning back from the course of the story to its starting-point – something which brings with it an interruption, naturally an arid and prosaic one, like any balance-sheet.

And how nasty, banal and useless the meaning of *any parable* is without the parable!

What the miracle of the saint has brought to the homestead moreover is none other than a large and many-coloured crowd of peasants: the same as one sees any Sunday in the shrines. The courtyards are so crowded that it is not easy to catch sight of Emilia seated there in the background. She has a black veil on her head that hides her green hair.

Along with the crowd a journalist has arrived with notebook and tape-recorder (perhaps even a reporter with a film-camera).

He – and one can read his bad conscience in his face – has evidently questions to ask of all those people and he looks around him for suitable 'people': there are poor housewives reddened by the cold and hard work, men destroyed by a life spent among the canals and riverbanks of the Plain under the thick mists, the icy low clouds and the weak suns; but there are also groups of the bourgeoisie, intellectuals, and (above all) ladies.

And it is precisely in connection with this journalistic investigation that the reader must undergo the violence –

perhaps unjustified violence – of an interpolation. It is the series of questions which the journalist puts to the people gathered in the courtyards of the farmstead: an interpolation which moreover belongs to a kind of language used in daily cultural commerce – in newspapers and in television – which is downright vulgar rather than trite. The questions in the investigation are more or less the following:

'Do you believe in miracles? And who performs them? God? And why? Why not to everyone or through everyone?'

*

'Do you believe that God only does miracles to those who believe or through those who truly believe?'

*

'If God revealed himself to you by means of a miracle do you think that you – your nature – would change? Or would you remain the same as before the miracle?'

*

'Do you think there would be a change in you? In that case would the miracle itself be more important or the change – brought about by the miracle in your human nature?'

*

'What is the reason, according to you, why God has chosen a poor woman of the people to reveal himself through this miracle?'

*

'Because the bourgeoisie cannot be truly religious?'

*

'Not in so far as they believe, or believe they believe, but in so far as they do not possess a real feeling for the sacred?'

*

'So even supposing the intervention of a miracle were to bring a member of the bourgeoisie perforce into the presence of something that is different, and therefore once more to question that *false idea of himself* which he has founded on so-called normality – could that person, in that case, arrive at a true religious feeling?'

*

'No? So in the members of the bourgeoisie every religious experience is reduced to a moral experience?'

*

'Moralism is the religion (when there is one) of the bourgeoisie?'

*

'So the bourgeoisie . . . *has replaced the soul with conscience*?'

*

'Every old religious situation is automatically transformed within him into a simple *case of conscience.*'

*

'So it is metaphysical religion that has been lost, transforming itself into a kind of *religion of good behaviour?*'

*

'So would this perhaps be the result of industrialization and of petty-bourgeois civilization?'

*

'So whatever happens to a member of the bourgeoisie, *even a miracle or an experience of divine love* could never awaken in him the ancient metaphysical feeling of the peasant ages? Becoming instead in him an arid struggle with his own conscience.'

*

'The soul has salvation as its aim – but the conscience?'

*

'God – in the name of whom this daughter of peasants who has returned from the city where she was a maid – does miracles – is the not an ancient God – to be precise a peasant one, biblical and a little mad?'

*

'And what sense does it make if his miracles take place in this surviving corner of a peasant world?'

*

'So religion survives today as an authentic fact only in the peasant world, that is to say . . . the Third World?'

*

'This mad saint at the gates of Milan within sight of the first factories – does she not mean this?'

*

'Is she not a terrible living accusation directed at the bourgeoisie which has (in the best of cases) reduced religion to a code of behaviour?'

*

'So while this peasant saint *can be saved* even if in an historical backwater, no member of the bourgeoisie, on the other hand, can be saved either as an individual or as a collective whole? As an individual, because he no longer has a soul but a conscience – a noble one perhaps but by its very nature coarse and limited; as a collective whole, because his history is running out without leaving traces, turning from being the history of the first industries to being the history of the complete industrialization of the world?'

*

'But the new type of religion which will be born then (and one can already see the first signs of it in the most advanced nations) will have nothing to do with this shit (excuse the word), which is the bourgeois, capitalist, or socialist world in which we live?'

*

16

THE MOMENT HAS COME TO DIE

It is very early. The sun has as yet to be born.

The homestead with its big courtyards is entirely deserted. At most there are some sparrows chirping in the frost. Only Emilia is there seated as always on her bench.

But there is a figure in black advancing uncertainly from the big door that gives on to the road – it is an old woman, a toothless old woman, sweet, as uncertain as a little girl, frightened by her own footsteps.

She is wearing her good dress, the one she wears on high days and holidays to go to early mass; and yet she comes in like a sneaking thief under the big gateway where it is still deep night and reappears on the threshold of the courtyard, still more uncertain, still more disorientated.

Perhaps she is afraid of having misunderstood, of having made a mistake, of having committed some error; and so, full of apprehension, she looks intently over to where the saint is seated, erect and inanimate. It is a long time before Emilia shows she has noticed her.

Then she gets up for the first time for so long; and, with the slow and obsessive step with which she had returned months and months before, joins the old woman who is waiting for her now with the reassured air of an accomplice.

Thus, together, the two women, without saying a word to each other begin their journey.

They re-enter the shadow of the big doorway and come out again further on in the light of the hazy expanses of the fields: here, however, instead of turning to the right along the tarred road, they continue along the cart-track that goes on into the countryside towards another white door (just like the one at the big entrance) which can just be made out in the still pale air.

The sun is on the horizon like a sad disc in the mist. Through the still colourless fields the two women, silent and in black, walk swiftly as though they were going to a distant market.

Emilia is weeping desperately and silently; but she allows these tears that gush out to run uninterrupted down her cheeks without drying them.

Around them the rural houses are becoming more numerous, surrounded by new estates: sad houses lit by a sun that reaches them in a troubled way, filtering through the mist that is still there far over the countryside.

When, on the other side of the green and oozing ditch by the country road a poster appears – as huge as the entire wall of a block of flats – on which a grey man, clenching his fist, announces that a new city will shortly rise in that district, Emilia quickens her pace, weeping and stern – and soon they reach a big asphalt road which, gleaming forlornly, leads to Milan.

With her old companion, who hobbles bravely behind her, Emilia, still shedding an unstoppable river of tears, is walking through the suburbs of Milan.

There is no life yet: everything stands still and composed as it did during the night in the cold bright moonlight.

*

The two travellers are walking in haste, not minding that their footsteps violate that silence of early dawn which is

159

respected by everything, men and things, as if in an unspoken pact. Only the sun is there and struggles, labouring wearily to invade the city once more with its eager and disconsolate light.

*

Having reached the spot she has chosen – or which she has found by chance and considered suitable for her plans – Emilia stops. And the old woman, without asking any questions, obedient as a child stops behind her .

Before then an enormous embankment opens up where a whole group of council flats is being built. At the centre of this embankment an excavator rises vertiginously: its jaws, in the inertia of this pre-dawn hour, are suspended and drooping against the sky.

Not far from the excavator is a hole – a very deep one; it is this that excavator has to fill. Emilia looks at that abyss with its dark muddy colour and makes up her mind: with slow and well-judged gestures she begins to climb down to the bottom, holding on to the pieces of turf sticking out of the earth, to the remaining bushes. Carefully, with the last of her energy, the old woman, like a peasant who has worked all her life without complaining, follows her; she does not argue with the saint's decisions, she considers them to be already laid down in heaven and in her simple old heart has decided that this is how things must be. The hole is fifteen or twenty metres deep and at the bottom the mud is still soft, gleaming with old puddles.

As purposeful and certain as an automaton but still weeping, Emilia lies down in the bottom of the hole against the steep wall. Then slowly, getting her faithful companion to help her, she sprinkles over herself a layer of mud so that, from above, she is invisible, melting into the soft gleaming soil and the puddles.

The tears which flow abundantly and without interruption, melting and mud only around her eyes, collect in a tiny puddle.

When Emilia is all covered with mud (and is now altogether unrecognizable, to the point of her being indistinguishable from the bottom of the hole), as if by tacit agreement the old woman leaves, climbing very slowly up the slippery path that brings her to the edge of the pit behind the rim of which she disappears.

*

The sun rises once more at last, with its tranquil splendour (as if all that chaotic and monstrous effort of the dawn had been a dream). Preceded by the chattering voices of men and by a few distant blows – far down the unechoing building sites – suddenly with a deafening screech – frightful, mad – the excavator wakens. But having uttered that first screech it is quiet. Silence descends once more, and the peace of the sun. But only for an instant for very soon the screeching begins again – and does not end. Lacerating, it every now and again follows the jerky and slow-witted movements of the machine which begins to move backwards and forwards as if animated by a will of its own although only capable of short and lunatic utterances – to gather up brutally an enormous quantity of earth in one place, to empty it out with a long screech of pain in another.

From the heap of mud that covers Emilia, tears continue to flow, in a real stream now, and the little puddle they have formed grows bigger.

*

The excavator has almost finished its task: the enormous hole at the bottom of which Emilia had concealed herself is no longer there. It is almost competely filled in with earth, still fresh and soft, which the excavator, finishing its labours and still screeching, continues to empty into the last remaining holes; but now all memory of the great hole seems to be lost.

At the place where Emilia has been buried (which by now would be difficult to identify), there begins to come out – slowly at first with the meticulous slowness of insects, then more and more impetuously – a thin jet of water: Emilia's tears – gradually they form a new little pool and from it a trickle of water begins to run across the earth.

It is at this point that alarmed cries are heard around and about – calls – weeping; then a confused noise of voices talking excitedly. From what part of the site are they coming? From the top floor empty to the sky? From the workshops in the open with their shuttering and reinforcing rods in the mud?

But the cries and voices seem to be nearer – in fact they come from behind a wooden fence that borders on the newly finished mound where buried Emilia's eyes make their tears gush out. And then from behind it – from behind the fence of new wood where a hand, a very crude one, has painted with dripping tar a hammer and sickle, a group of workers appears.

They come over the soft earth at a hasty pace, continuing to speak excitedly. Among them one makes his way with difficulty, supported by his comrades who hold up one of his arms as delicately as possible. The arm is bloody and the wounded man is looking around him as he walks in terror.

When, almost at a run, the group is close to the little pool of tears, one of his helpers sees it, stops and, pushing him, brings the wounded man to it; he dips his hands in it like a scoop and with that water, without giving it a thought (he is a poor old man who certainly comes from the countryside), he washes the wound on his companion's wrist and hand.

No sooner does the water begin to wash the blood from the flesh than the wound also begins to heal; in a few seconds the cut closes and the blood stops flowing.

Before the workmen, as is natural, begin to raise their shouts of astonishment – giving themselves over to the naïve and slightly silly demonstrations which men cannot restrain when faced by things of which they have no experience – there is a moment of profound silence. Their poor faces, hollowed, hard and good, are turned towards that little pool which gleams inconceivably in the sun.

17

PAOLO'S COROLLARY

The father, Paolo, comes out of the villa, gets into his Mercedes and he too takes the road down which the guest disappeared one day.

One like the other, the squares and avenues follow on from each other on all sides beyond his car-windows in the leaden grey which alternates every so often at the most hostile and anonymous spots, with a certain miserable sweet sunlight. Unprotected, in that powerful car of his, Paolo goes through the centre of the city, searching. It is the time of day when he is usually at work; and in fact all Milan is at work. But he, on the contrary, *is searching*, not bound by any rules or time-tables.

Like his wife Lucia, Paolo has come to terms with life – how much so and how unwittingly! And so his way of losing it cannot be other than a coming to terms, however irrational and abject. Yet the glances of someone searching are always the same whatever that person is searching for. And Paolo's eyes as he looks around him – in that city which wishes him to be the same as everyone else and, into the bargain, sure of himself, an arrogant boss – are so pleading, as if hurt, so anxious, that the bargain he has struck with his life *so as to be able to lose it* has also about it something extremist and pure.

*

He has arrived at the piazza in front of the Central Station:

here work is going on and it is difficult to park the car. He drives about, in a state of anxiety, childishly infuriated (an old habit) with all the other men: those marvellous inferiors who sagely and unconsciously people life. At last he finds a space, leaves the car there. He gets out, hiding his face as much as possible with the collar of his coat, scared, longing, brutal behind a mask of an excessive calm.

He goes into the station and wanders about for a while through the halls of the ticket office (he has the excuse of buying newspapers and consulting the departures timetable). And meantime he is looking around him, pretending that there is nothing the matter, *searching*. Then, like the dozens and dozens of anonymous persons who have the same anxious desire for dignity, he walks towards the escalator, goes up it, and here he is among the milky spaces of the enormous vault of the cantilever roof. In this world, which is a kind of limbo, Paolo's uncertainty increases, becomes almost a panic. Where to go? How to justify himself in a place where everyone has a precise reason for being there? He tries, it is true, to pretend to be a citizen waiting for members of his family or friends arriving on some train or other: but he has to *search* and therefore wander about, move about, compromise himself: this is something more important than his dignity.

The miracle happens to him, as always, when he touches the bottom: in fact Paolo finds himself, desperate by now, on the least crowded and least well-lit platform that runs along the left-hand wall with its row of forlorn doorways right down to the end of the huge iron arch where the light of the sky appears (and the reader must be satisfied with this hint which does not say everything – but ours is a report written with timidity and fear).

The two blue eyes of a face that turns round, looking over

the wide shoulders, are those of a youth sitting miserably on a bench: perhaps an unemployed person who has long hours to pass alone, waiting for something to happen, or simply a workman waiting, as patient as a conscript soldier, for his local train.

They are two eyes full of goodness and innocence.

Paolo stops behind him, literally trembling for sure. He begins to force himself to read the newspaper and, following his plan, looks up every so often. What he is hoping for is that the youth will turn round again. But the boy seems to be lost in a state of absent-mindedness like a somnolent animal; who knows what thoughts, what plans for the future he has in his head, and in what place of dreams his life unfolds.

The minutes pass and the boy does not turn round; while behind him Paolo makes every effort to pretend to be – although with difficulty – someone almost severe and rigid although a little anxious: so much so as not to be able to keep his attention for more than a few seconds on his newspaper.

The two blue eyes, good, innocent, and now a little alarmed, suddenly turn round and come to a halt on the eyes of Paolo who replies to that glance in an almost hostile way, incapable of any reaction.

Some more minutes pass, many of them. Then, as if in a dream, the boys gets up. Is everything over? Do things resolve themselves so bitterly and with such clarity?

He is tall, robust (and good, innocent, even in the build of his body. Yes, a conscript a twenty-year-old dressed in his poor bourgeois way).

Will he go off now without turning round?

Very slowly Paolo realizes that he is making for the far end of the vaulted roof (where there is the white light of the sky) and that it is not true that he does not turn round: before passing through the forlorn doorway a little further on, he in fact fleetingly looks back once more, with his blue eyes, charged with light and empty of any expression.

Paolo moves on too – he takes a few steps in the murky light of the station – goes uncertainly towards that little door – but then stops suddenly.

We shall not even try to enter into Paolo's consciousness – just as we did not enter the consciousness of Lucia. We shall confine ourselves to describing his actions which are due – that is evident – to a consciousness that is already outside life.

As if overcome and grateful for it, he begins carefully to take off his fine light overcoat, a faultless product of English manufacture, lets it fall to his feet, where it flops like a dead thing or something that has suddenly become unconnected with him; the same fate befalls his jacket, followed by his tie, his pullover, his shirt.

Paolo stands there bare-chested on the station platform and the few people who are moving about in these parts at this dead hour began to stop and look at him. What is happening to that man?

Now cut off from everything, Paolo continues, undaunted and far away, to strip himself of what he is wearing, almost as if he could not distinguish reality from its symbols; or else, perhaps, as if he had decided to cross, once and for all, the vain and illusory boundaries which divide reality from its representation. Something, in short, that men do when some faith detaches them for ever from their lives.

So on top of all the other clothes there fall first his vest, then his trousers, his underpants, his socks, his shoes. Alongside the heap of clothes there finally appear his two bare feet: which turn round and at a slow pace go away, along the grey and shining pavement of the platform amid the crowd of people, who are shod, and who press round him, alarmed and silent.

18

INVESTIGATION INTO THE DONATION
OF THE FACTORY

The midday bells are ringing from nearby Lainate or from Arese, still nearer. With them the sirens mingle.

The factory stretches the whole length of the horizon, like an immense raft anchored among the canals and the transparent barriers of poplars.

The atmosphere is elegiac; these two or three kilometres of horizontal walls, softened by the light mist, with tenderness and Lombard brightness, 'Calm, luxury and sensual pleasure.'[1] Even the hundreds upon hundreds of cars standing in rows in the car-parks seem to be only the coloured tesselations of that order and that peace.

Suddenly it is all hell broken loose: the six thousand five hundred workers from the factory begin to come out together, spewed out by the fragile gates and the expanses of the car-parks are overwhelmed as if by a cyclone.

And yet the spaces in front of the factory are immense and spreading over it, the crowd of workmen thins out. And very soon would end up by thinning out altogether if small groups, in clumps, were not forming here and there, unexpectedly and contrary to all the rules, as on those days when some strike is being planned or before the elections. There are also squads of police, watchful and sly, while members of the

---

[1] A slight misquotation from Baudelaire's *L'Invitation au voyage* which has the refrain 'luxe, calme et volupté' (Tr.).

bourgeoisie – evidently journalists or people who are curious – mix with the workers.

The reader must at this point, for the second time, put up as patiently as possible with a new insertion into the story – use the pedal of the power of everyday logic, abandoning with understandable disappointment that of the sweet imagination.

In fact a journalist – or reporter with his film-camera (perhaps the same one as at Emilia's farmstead) confronts the crowd of workers with a professional air that does not mask either his timidity or his bad conscience; and he begins to ask them the questions he has carefully prepared in his low-grade language, that of the average citizens' culture.

Here, more or less, are those questions designed to bring us back as sharply to the squalid prose of the here and now, without which in any case neither the author nor the reader – united in a tacit and guilty alliance – would be able to have a conscience at peace:

'You are a worker who works here? For how many years? And you? Well, what do you think of what your boss has done?'

*

'He has donated his factory to you workers – now you are the owners – but are you not humiliated by the fact of having received this donation?'

*

'Would you not have preferred to obtain your right to power over the factory by means of an action taken by yourselves?'

*

'In all this is the chief actor not still your boss? And so has he put you in the shade? Has he not somehow cut you off from your revolutionary future?'

*

'But is your boss's act an isolated one or rather, does it represent a general tendency among all the bosses of the modern world?'

*

'Where will participation in power over the factory, obtained by a series of donations – or rather of concessions – take the working-class?'

*

'Would the transformation of man into a petty-bourgeois be total?'

*

'So if we take this donation as a symbol or an extreme case of the new direction of power, does it not end up by presenting itself as a first, pre-historic contribution to the transformation of all men into petty-bourgeois?'

*

'As public act, then, the donation of the factory would be –

at least from the point of view of the workers and the intellectuals – a historical crime and, as a private act, an old religious solution?'

*

'But is this religion solution not the survival of a world which no longer has anything to do with ours? Is it not born of guilt rather than of love? So that a member of the bourgeoisie would never be able to find his life again were he to lose it?'

*

'The hypothesis – not a very original one – would therefore be that the bourgeoisie can no longer, in any way, free itself from its fate, neither publicly nor privately and that *whatever a member of the bourgeoisie does is wrong*?'

*

'Can one consider the cause of all this to be the idea of possession and of preservation?'

*

'But are the ideas of possession and of preservation on which the condemnation of the bourgeoisie is based not characteristic of the old world of the bosses? While the new world is not so much concerned with *possessing and preserving* as with *producing and consuming*?'

*

171

'If it was the ancient peasant world that lent the emerging bourgeoisie – in the times when it was founding its first industries – the desire to possess and preserve *but not its religious feeling*, was not all the indignation and all the anger against it justified?'

*

'But if that bourgeoisie is now changing its nature in a revolutionary manner and has a tendency to force the whole of humanity to be like itself until there is a complete identification of the bourgeois individual with man, have that anger and that ancient indignation not lost all meaning?'

*

'And if the bourgeoisie – identifying itself with the whole of humanity – no longer has anyone outside itself on whom to lay the burden of its own condemnation (which it has never been able nor willing to pronounce) *has this ambiguity not at last become a tragedy*?'

*

'A tragedy because, no longer having a class struggle to win – by any means, even criminal ones, like the idea of the Nation, of the Army, of the Confessional Church – it remains alone, faced by the necessity of knowing what it itself is?'

*

'If it is victorious – at least potentially – and the future belongs to it – is it not up to it itself to reply now (and no longer to the forces of struggle and revolution) to the questions which history – which is *its story* – poses?'

'CAN IT NOT REPLY TO THESE QUESTIONS?'

19

'OH, MY NAKED FEET . . .'

Oh my naked feet that are walking
across the desert sand.
My naked feet that are bearing me
where there is only one presence
and where there is nothing to shield me from any
    glance!
My naked feet
that have decided on a path
which I now follow as in a vision
like that of the fathers who built,
in the Twenties, my villa in Milan and of the young
architects who finished it in 1960!
As once for the people of Israel or the apostle Paul,
the desert appears to me
as that part of reality that is alone indispensable.
Or better still as the reality
quite stripped (except of its essence)
just as a person imagines it who lives and sometimes
thinks it but without being a philosopher.
In fact, all around, there is nothing
except what is necessary:
the earth, the sky and the body of a man.
However mad, abysmal or ethereal
the dark horizon may be, its line is ONE:
and any of its points is the same as any other point.
The dark desert that seems to shine,

such is its sugary purity
and the cavity of the sky, incurably blue, that
constantly change but remain the same.
Good. And what of me?
Of me, who am where I was and was where I am,
the automaton of a real person,
dispatched into the desert to walk through it?
I AM FILLED BY A QUESTION WHICH NO ONE CAN
    ANSWER.
Sad result, if I have chosen this desert
as the real and true place of my life!
Is he who was searching in the streets of Milan
the same as the one who now searches on the roads of the
    desert?
It is true: the symbol of reality
has something reality does not have:
it does not represent any meaning
and yet it adds to it – by its very
representative nature – a new meaning.
But – certainly not as for the people of Israel or the apostle
    Paul –
this new meaning remains indecipherable to me.
In the profound silence of the sacred evocation
I then ask myself if, by going into the desert,
I must not have had a life
already predestined to the desert and if, therefore,
living in the days of history – so much less beautiful,
pure and essential than its representation –
I ought not to have been able to reply
to its infinite and useless questions
in order to be able, now, to reply
to this desert, unique and absolute.
Wretched, prosaic conclusion –

a lay one because of the imposition of a culture of
     oppressed people –
of a process begun in order to lead to God!
But what will prevail? The mundane aridity
of reason or religion, despicable
fecundity of one who lives left behind by history?
So my face is sweet and resigned
when I walk slowly –
exhausted and dripping with sweat
when I run –
filled with a sacred terror
when I look around this endless oneness –
childishly worried
when I watch under my naked feet
the sand on which I slip or clamber.
Just as in my life, as in Milan.
But why do I unexpectedly stop?
Why do I gaze ahead of me as if I saw something?
While there is nothing new other than the dark horizon
which stands out infinitely different and similar
against the blue sky of this place
imagined by my poor civilization?
Why, against my will,
does my face contract, the veins
in my neck swell,
my eyes fill with a fiery light?
And why does the scream which a few moments later
comes raging from my throat
not add anything to the ambiguity which up to now
has dominated this walk of mine through the desert?
It is impossible to say what my scream
is like; it is true that it is terrible –
so terrible as to disfigure my lineaments

making them the jaws of a beast –
but it is also somehow joyous –
so joyous as to reduce me to almost a child.
It is a scream made to attract the attention of someone,
or his help; but perhaps also to curse him.
It is a scream that wants to let it be known
in this uninhabited spot *that I exist*,
or else that I not only exist
but that I know. It is a scream
in which behind the fear
one hears a certain craven accent of hope:
or else a scream of certainty, absolutely absurd,
in which there is the pure sound of despair.
In any case this is certain: that whatever
this scream of mine tries to say
it is fated to last beyond any possible end.

APPENDICES

With reference to chapter 6, part one ('End of Exposition'):

Le jeune homme, dont l'oeil est brillant, la peau brune,
Le beau corps de vingt ans qui devrait aller nu,
Et qu'eût, le front cerclé de cuivre, sous la lune
Adoré, dans la Perse, un Génie inconnu,

  Impétueux avec des douceurs virginales
Et noires, fier de ses premiers entêtements,
Pareil aux jeunes mers . . .

(From *Poésies* by Rimbaud)

With reference to chapter 14, part one ('Re-education to Disorder and Disobedience'):

'*Before I formed thee in the belly I knew thee*; [a knowledge which also implies, as is well known, physical love] *and before thou camest forth out of the womb I sanctified thee,* and *I ordained thee a prophet unto the nations.*

  Then said I, Ah, Lord GOD! behold, I cannot speak: for I am a child.' [The emphasis is ours.]

  '*But the LORD said unto me, Say not, I am a child: for thou shalt go to all that I shall send thee, and whatsoever I command thee thou shalt speak.*

  Be not afraid of their faces: for I am with thee to deliver thee, said the LORD.

  Then the LORD put forth his hand, and touched my mouth. And the LORD said unto me, Behold, I have put my words in thy mouth.'

(From Jeremiah 1: 5–9)

With reference to chapters 16 and 17, part one ('It is the Father's Turn' and 'Entirely Miraculous like Morning Light Never Seen Before'):

And Jacob was left alone; and a man [or God] *wrestled with him until day break. When the man saw that he could not prevail against Jacob, he touched the hollow of his thigh; and Jacob's thigh was put out of joint as he wrestled with him. Then he said: 'Let me go for it is day break.'*

(From Genesis 32: 24)

With reference to chapter 22, part one ('Through the Eyes of the Father in Love'), the passage by Rimbaud which the guest is reading is probably this:

'She [in our case 'he'] *belonged to her own life; and goodness's turn would take longer to reproduce itself than a star. The Adorable Person who, without my having ever hoped it, had come, did not return and will return no more.'*

With reference to the whole statement (or as it says in the text 'report'):

'O LORD, thou hast deceived me, and I was deceived: thou art stronger than I, and hast prevailed: I am in derision daily, every one mocketh me . . .

For I heard the defaming of many, fear on every side. Report, say they, and we will report it. All my familiars watched for my halting, saying, Peradventure he will be enticed, and we shall prevail against him, and we shall take our revenge on him.'

(From Jeremiah 20: 7, 10)